The Dilemmas of Contemporary Religion

The Dilemmas of
Contemporary Religion

by

D. A. MARTIN

ST. MARTIN'S PRESS
NEW YORK

Library of Congress Cataloging in Publication Data

Martin, David A
The dilemmas of contemporary religion.

Includes bibliographical references.
CONTENTS: Christianity, civic religion, and three
counter-cultures. – Traditional religion and the traditional
transitions to the tradition of the new. – Institutionalism
and community. – Mutations, religio-political crisis and
the collapse of Puritanism and humanism. [etc.]
1. Religion – Addresses, essays, lectures. I. Title.
BL50.M323   209   78-17704
ISBN 0-312-21055-8

Contents

Acknowledgements

Chapter   I – appeared in *Human Context*, Vol. VI, No. 3, 1974.

Chapter II – was given at Jerusalem on the occasion of the centenary of the Hebrew Union College, April 1976.

Chapter III – first appeared in the *Acts of the Twelfth Conference of the Sociology of Religion*, The Hague, 1973, published by C.I.S.R., Lille, and then subsequently in *The Month*, December 1973.

Chapter IV – was given at a conference in Venice in October 1973 and was printed in Paul Seabury (ed.), *Universities in the Western World*, The Free Press, Collier-Macmillan, 1975.

Chapter V – was originally written at St. Davids during Easter 1971 and then reformulated for a conference in Oxford with Eastern European professors of scientific atheism in September 1976. It so happened they were unable to come.

Chapter VI – was given at Jouy-en-Josas, and appeared in G. Suffert (ed.), *Les Terreurs de l'an 2000*, Hachette 1976.

'Not merely was Jesus Christ the Son of God, but he came of very good family on his mother's side, and there are excellent reasons for seeing in him the legitimate heir to the throne of Judah.'

Sermon preached before Charles X (1829)

In every way it has come to this, that what one now calls Christianity is precisely what Christ came to abolish. This has happened especially in Protestantism, and especially among the Grundtvigians.

The Grundtvigians are in fact in the strictest sense Jews. I undertake to prove that they have such a Jewish conception of marriage that they do not merely, as in Christianity, regard it as permissible (in contrast to celibacy), nor as a *diaphoron*: no, they believe that one cannot be a proper Christian without being married, that a flock of children and a numerous posterity are a blessing of God and a sign that God is well pleased – an entirely Jewish conception.

Further, in place of circumcision they have baptism (again an objective matter) to which they appeal just as the Jews do to circumcision.

Further, a right Jewish superstition about descent.

Further, the illusion that they are God's chosen people, either simply that the Christians (the baptized) are God's chosen people, or that the Danes are.

This is Jewish optimism, the most dangerous sort of epicurism, that, namely, which turns enjoyment of this life into religion.

And this is supposed to be New Testament Christianity!

XI'A 149 Kierkegaard
Protestantism, especially à la Grundtvig

Introduction

This short book contains several long books which I will never write. Almost all the pieces are highly concentrated therefore. They provide the structure of an argument and the illustrations are lightly pencilled *en passant*.

My recent book on secularization[1] was concerned with the empirical fortunes of religious institutions and to a much lesser extent of beliefs. It was written therefore in a generalizing mode and in the form of a continuous argument. However, that institutional level is only part of the social reality and those empirical trends need to be subsumed in a much wider and more comprehensive socio-logic. Indeed, they are also infiltrated by a logic of symbols which I will discuss in a further volume.

Each of these essays is concerned with a very general kind of socio-logic and constitutes a variety of meta-history. I concentrate on the logic of Christianity and of Judaism and try to exhibit the character of their mutual relationship. Every expression of human aspiration must include some element of unfreedom: there is no variety of socio-logic which allows all the gains and none of the costs. Only the isolated intellectual can invent a costless world. Christianity and Judaism are two closely related kinds of socio-logic, close enough and different enough to react on each other. On a continuum of all possible socio-logics they are adjacent. In other words they are as logically similar as they are historically intertwined. The position is complicated by the fact that Christianity generates counter-cultures from within itself, such as monasticism, Protestant dissent and existentialism, while Judaism is structurally pushed into the counter-cultural role. So Christendom contains several explosive elements, which include both the logical implications of its own deposit of faith, and the social implications and consequences of Jewish marginality. The first essay largely explores the varied counter-cultural styles of Christianity while the second explores the dialectic of Christianity and Judaism (or rather, Jewishness). The fifth essay on Marxism is an examination of a crucial mutation of the socio-logic of Christianity and Judaism, and takes up the concluding observations of the second essay.

Essays three and four are concerned with a somewhat different dialectic, which is that between external institutions and spontaneous forms, either the spontaneous community or the pure interiority of autonomous selfhood. The third essay turns on the counterpoint between rational, large-scale structures and direct, personal, affective, involvement in communal attachments. The fourth essay places this counterpoint in the context of the student movement where pure selfhood attacked the mental disciplines of humanism and psychic disciplines of Puritanism. Of course humanism and Puritanism are as much threatened by bureaucracy as they are by the vagaries of the naked self. (I have discussed those particular vagaries elsewhere, notably in Chapters 5 and 12 of my *Tracts Against the Times*.)[2]

The last essay was written when I was completing my work on the general theory of secularization. This means that it reflects more directly on that general theory and is more clearly in the empirical style. *Religion and the Second Millennium* was written in response to an invitation to reflect on the likely future of political ideology and religion once the terrors of the year 2000 were upon us.

Notes

1. *A General Theory of Secularisation*, Blackwell, 1978.
2. *Tracts Against the Times*, Lutterworth Press, 1973.

I

Christianity, Civic Religion and Three Counter-Cultures[1]

I am going to begin by suggesting a contrast between civic religion, which expresses the unity of religion and society postulated by Durkheim, and a Christian dialectic which infiltrates and transcends that unity. This dialectic has a Catholic form, a Protestant form and maybe also a Post-Protestant form. In the first the monks choose the holy community, in the second the believer chooses a relationship to the holy individual, and in the last the rebel sacralizes the notion of choice *per se*.[2] This creates counter-cultures above and below the unity of the natural society; it initiates breaks in the natural community of tradition and generation; and it generates double meanings and parallel motifs to those of natural language. In that sense it is supernatural. (Above all, the Christian dialectic takes the central words of the natural society – Kingdom, Power and Peace – which are the vocabulary of social hierarchy and consensus, and transmutes them into the coinage of a different realm: Christianity is the most profound form of the *double entendre*. 'He that hath ears to hear let him hear.') This area of double meanings, parallel motifs and inverted images is very important since it works not only in counter-cultures but throughout society. Unfortunately it is too extensive a topic to be developed here.

Civic religion has two manifestations. The first is a straightforward Durkheimian unity of cult and culture, in which religion and culture are isomorphic and where the existing hierarchy of social positions is largely coextensive with and legitimated by religion. The paradigm case is that of the sacred emperor. This type of religion is inherently conserving in its tendency and secular in that 'whatever is, is right'. The given, socially, is the ultimate. The secular has sucked the divine into its maw. The second manifestation is the *mélange* of superstition, astrology, proverbial morality and accepted limited personal reciprocities currently comprising the natural religion of our time and which has persisted as an undertow in Christian (and other) cultures for millennia. It is secular in quite another sense: not only does it express the local tangle of involvements but it also uses *pragmatic* criteria in its judgement of religious efficacy. The two forms of civic religion both represent power: the one is the social *power* and the established glory, the other is the power of what works. What socially *is* and what pragmatically *works* represent underlying secularity. But the dynamic ambiguity of Christianity remains, breaking up these homogeneities and inertias and then succumbing to them. Its power and its glory is both of and not of this world: it makes whole and holy; what supremely *is* consists of a power made perfect in weakness and rejection. Not only are kings crowned but so are saints and martyrs. There is a crucial feminine element embodied in the worship of Mary and her Child, in the *theologia crucis*, and in the social gospel of peace.

I am going to argue that my three counter-cultures and their alternative conceptual coinage have to find a lodgement over against civic religion, which varies according to the type of society concerned, whether for example it is feudal in its organization, or an absolutist nation state or a semi-pluralistic liberal society. The absolutist nation state, because of the tremendous centripetal force of its unitary organization and consciousness, creates the most difficult challenge for counter-cultures and double meanings. Moreover, the degree to which it is successful creates social moulds which shape the possibilities for future counter-cultures. If the unitary mould hardens too rigidly, society tends to split into two cultures in mutual and permanent antagonism: this is the French situation since 1789. Or alternatively the unitary force may be so strong that when rapid change comes, the system simply turns over on its back with its fundamental rigidity undisturbed: for example, Russia in 1917. An entirely opposite possibility is realized in America. The state and religion both become federal: the centre does not hold. The British and Scandinavian patterns are intermediate in their degree of unity. In Britain the absolutist baroque state fails and a relatively weak centre confronts a partly autonomous counter-culture initiated by Protestant dissent. In Scandinavia the baroque state is successful but there remain varying possibilities for counter-culture. The periphery has some opportunity to confront the centre.

It is on the social margins that the dialectic finds its base: whether it is the monastic margin in feudal society or the cultures of geographical and social marginality in liberal society. The Durkheimian unity of religion and society faces a frequent alliance between the dialectic of Christianity and cultural marginality. Moreover, this alliance brings with it a paradox. The dialectic poses change against tradition, choice against involuntary nature. The community it posits is based on choice, not generation. But the culture of a margin, especially of a margin under pressure, may need to defend its *own* stability and tradition, even against choice. The dialectic finds a base but that base can only be partly occupied. This is because the base reflects the enemy against which it is directed, and because every success creates a correlative failure. Monasteries become wealthy bastions of the system they attack; free churches become stagnant pools of tradition. Therefore counter-cultures have to be followed by different counter-cultures: a dialectic within the dialectic. I shall, therefore, be concerned with a sequence of counter-cultures each strongly directed not only against the centre but against the previous counter-culture: Protestant dissent attacking the monastic principle, the student movement attacking the Protestant ethic. The new base-camp assaults the old base-camp. Yet each will still be joined thematically to the other against the centre, affirming the community of choice, eroding the notion of hierarchy, subverting the masculine and civic ideals of the power and the glory.

Let us explore further the Christian dialectic. The Christian relationship with culture either creates communities of choice alongside and within the natural community or it sets the choosing individual over against society. In this sense it must be seen as inherently pluralistic and voluntaristic: it disrupts the identity of religion and society. That is one reason why it differs from Judaism, and one reason why it seeks to convert. A converting religion is a chosen religion. The communities of choice it creates are either monastic or they are sects and denominations which are separated from the natural community, even though, through the socialization of succeeding generations, they eventually become quasi-naturalistic. These free associations may form both within and outside a state church: they affirm personal commitment and lay participation. And of course there is the choice of the solitary individual over against all structures, of which the supreme example is a Søren Kierkegaard.

Between the dialectic of the monks and that of Protestant dissent stands the absolute state, inimical to all centrifugal tendencies and to all religious dialectic. Here the dialectic goes underground and burrows at the level of psychology: it creates parallel motifs to those of secular culture. If the power of kings is displayed in vast secular palaces, then the power of the King of Kings is displayed in palatial churches. Erotic love is paralleled by the mystical wounds of divine love and by the visitation of the heavenly bridegroom: in Bernini's St. Teresa, in St. John of the Cross, in the poetry of a Crashaw or Angelus Silesius.

This notion of the community of choice is to be expanded below, but reference to the nation state reminds us that the natural community is never without its victories. Out of the Christian forms it creates and selects a content subservient to its functional requirements and to the permanent centripetal force of hierarchy, order, coercion and social power. There appear versions of Christianity in Republican America, Republican France, Republican Florence and Whig England which are predominantly civic in tone. Robert Bellah labelled the American version 'The Civic Religion of America'. Hans Baron, writing of Florence, called it 'Civic Humanism'. There is even an affiliated variant in contemporary folk-religiosity. One can rapidly envisage what this involves by considering the ethos of Republican France, and its re-creation of Ancient Roman models. Consider only those stern exemplars of stoic duty, based on Roman originals, to be found in the pictures of David. To appreciate this ethos musically one should listen to the tremendous anthems Handel wrote for the Coronation of George II or Berlioz's *Grande Messe des Morts*, which he declared a fitting requiem for Napoleon.

Such a religion plays down the theme of salvation because that arouses a tension with the natural community, and it extols stoic devotion to the ideals of citizenship. It sets remembered classics against pondered Scripture, even-handed justice against divine grace, city fathers against fathers in God, the continuing life of immortality against the abruptness of Resurrection. The community of generation is concerned with remembrance and continuity. A Remembrance Day is its most solemn feast: the redemption of a nation by a collective sacrifice. Having a preference for the military virtues it values suffering not as the saving expression of universal love but largely as a prerequisite of '*la gloire*', the proper duty required in the last resort of a citizen: *sed miles, sed pro patria*. This religion recognizes power and, therefore, refers with ceremonial deference and Churchillian rhetoric to the Almighty. The Almighty represents, after all, a broad enough notion to meet the consensus of most sensible men and the needs of the national front. Happily the Lord of Hosts is not implicated in the attitude to Caesar and to warfare advocated by His Son. Hence on the walls of Anglican churches and of the school chapel the moral law and mannerly decencies take over. Religion grows Ciceronian. The ten commandments, symbolic of cosmic law and order, dominate the altars of love and sacrifice. The churches of central London are the splendid, light-filled temples of a rational civic cult.

But if Christianity is guardian of a plural and voluntary dialectic then it decays internally when made too easily amenable to the ideals of republics and nations, as witness the fate of eighteenth-century Anglicanism. Of course the reassertion of a dialectic cannot occur in an ideal form but must seize what limited openings are available within given types of social structure. We can now consider these openings as utilized by Catholicism in relation to late feudal society and by Protestantism in relation to incipiently plural liberal society.

Catholicism creates communities above and below the state which from time to time diverge from the norms of civilization, meaning by that the good natural life of the best type of man, concerned with earthly justice, and with a full existence in terms of the pleasures of food, art and family. The vehicles of the Catholic thrust above and below the state are the monastic orders, dedicated like a fifth column within to the supreme state without, i.e. to the Roman obedience. Likewise the ordinary clergy strive to acquire a lever of independence and succeed in becoming a separate estate with some measure of internal regulation. Now both monks and clergy by their partial success are condemned to mirror the system against which they succeed. The clergy become a separate feudal estate. The monastic protest against wealth grows both more extreme and more relaxed, because the consequence of the protest is landed, corporate wealth on a vast scale. The meek find it curiously easy to inherit the earth. Each wave of reform recognizes this by a more extreme assertion of poverty. Like the voluntary free churches later the monks cannot avoid corporate social mobility. It is this, of course, which weakens them as moral exemplars and arouses the envy of kings.

Yet what the Catholic system achieved is best appreciated if we compare the monks and priests of Catholicism with the eunuchs of oriental despotisms. Monks were elected celibates, whereas eunuchs were such without choice. The eunuchs constituted a peculiarly dependent and dependable Civil Service and they were movable according to the logic and needs of the realm not the logic and needs of a supranational, Universal Church.

Kings, attempting to assert or recover the Durkheimian unity of Church and state, religion and society, invariably turn against monk and pope, not merely because of rapacity and not simply because pope and monk have themselves become rapacious, but because together they represent an expression of the social dualism of Christianity. Throughout the late Middle Ages, in England and Scandinavia as elsewhere, King is ambivalent to Church and vice versa. According to Ernest Barker that struggle is the most profound in history, although we now find it difficult to see why it took the particular form which it did.

As Harald III of Norway put it from the kingly viewpoint, 'I know no archbishop or ruler in Norway save myself.' The great exemplar of this struggle is, of course, Thomas à Becket, himself reflecting the system in his feudal pride and worldliness, but standing firm to martyrdom on the principle of the state within the state, refusing to combine Civil Service and Church, asserting a law beyond the law.

Thus the empirical forms of Christian social dualism within the feudal system are inevitably also feudal in character: a semi-independent estate within a hierarchy of estates, an independent *état* Rome, inserted in the comity of monarchies and dukedoms, but in a sense just another monarchy. But below these social forms were the psychological bases of the state within and above the state: the celibacy of the clergy and the elevation of the Virgin. Clerical celibacy and the Marian devotion are locked together in logic and psychology because they assert a symbolic break in communities of generation and a softening of the male ethos by which they are dominated. Similarly, the Virgin Birth of Christ affirms a new beginning by spiritual generation, not mere repetitive physical procreation. Natural communities are rooted in the never-ending cycle of generation, not in choice: the clergy reject generation for themselves and *choose* to belong to their estate. This is another reason why it allows them a social mobility which is closed off when kings assert their rights of appointment and make the church hierarchy a simple reflection of the social system.

Catholicism creates a complete spiritual family outside the system of generation: the Holy Father, the monastic brothers, the motherhood of Mary. This then affects the male avocation of arms in an extraordinary way through the psychology of chivalry: the figure of 'the parfit, gentil knight'. The devotion of the valiant male, properly directed to his wife, shifts to the spiritual adoration of a lady who is *not* his wife and to our Lady, both his lady and our Lady being outside the cycle of generation. Our Lady moves parallel to our Lord, thus complementing the system of lords and ladies at exactly the same time as it breaks it. St. Bernard is perhaps the great example of the way the celibate turns towards the Virgin Mother and breaks the cycle of generation, reinterpreting the erotic Jewish poetry of the Song of Songs in a spiritual sense. So when kings eventually assert themselves against monk and pope they often reassert the cycle of generation by abolishing celibacy and the Virgin. They thus recover the unity of their realms, and of present and past, and can locate a more direct analogue of their power in a worship of the Almighty Father. After all, it was Henry VIII, that atrocious exemplar of rampant maleness, who attacked pope and monk over a question of a succeeding generation.

If we turn from this Catholic system of tensions to the position of Protestantism activating and expressing an incipiently plural society, we find quite a different concatenation of motifs, though with important links with the Catholic past, such as the continuing devotion to the atoning grace of the Saviour. I shall develop that important continuity later, as well as the theme of feminization – which is taken up after a significant break. That break is the period of the absolute nation state. It may be important that the period of the absolute state is also the great period of mysticism, a private concession to the feminine principle in which the single individual is chosen and passive rather than choosing. Thus, as I have said, the current of the dialectic runs under the edifice of the visible church: voluntarism becomes cryptic.

The logic of Protestantism is clearly in favour of voluntary principle, to a degree that eventually makes it sociologically unrealistic. It affirms personal choice or, in its original form, God's choice of the person. Luther's conception of a real invisible Church distinct from the extant empirical organization is crucial as a dogmatic base from which pluralism and choice can be extended. This can be developed into the notion that true believers can be united across organizations and national boundaries. But there are a whole variety of ways in which the Protestant principle can be realized according to the particular logic of the form of Protestantism embraced and according to the social base available. In Kierkegaard for example we have an extreme case: the individual affirms the either/or of Christianity against the state Church and unitary state, against the Hegelian celebration of the embodiment of the Spirit in civil society, against the local Danish version of cultural Christianity propagated by Grundvig. Naturally he forms no continuing organizational tradition. Existential choice cannot propagate itself naturalistically. All other versions of Protestantism must concede something to sociological necessity, particularly, of course, if their voluntarism is linked to the protest of a local culture with special interest in survival. After all we are considering counter-*cultures*.

The most notable realization of the dialectic of choice is the concept of Protestant dissent and it is, therefore, unsurprising that what is continuous with monasticism as an *alternative* expression of the dialectic should also be most strongly opposed to the monastic principle. Protestant dissent depends for its viability on some break in the unitary state, some base for expanding against the old cultural centre, some locus for secondary élites to confront the old primary élites.

It comes in three waves, each achieving a group mobility

analogous to the corporate mobility of monks, but beginning at lower and lower points in the status system. This movement corresponds to the shifting extension of democratization and is accompanied by an accelerated emotionalism with each step downwards in social status. The Calvinistic wave begins fairly high in the scale and mounts high enough in some cases to overwhelm the primary élite and constitute a new centre: Holland, Scotland, Switzerland. In other places it forms a high-status secondary élite which is part of the active innovating sector of a society, as in England and – when not subject to persecution – in France. In America, where a universal voluntarism is established, Calvinist dissent cannot form a new centre not can it be described as a secondary élite. It simply takes its place as a culture which is *primus inter pares*. At any rate there are no instances where the first and most successful wave of dissent stands lower in the social scale than the second wave, i.e. Methodism and its affiliated variants.

Methodism corresponds to the awakening culture of the small artisan, minor entrepreneur and (sometimes) the small farmer. It forms a substantial band of autonomy in Anglo-Saxon cultures but rarely achieves the status of a secondary élite and never overwhelms a primary élite. Wherever Calvinism dominated the commanding heights of culture the counter-culture of Methodism found a secure lodgement difficult to achieve, for example, in Scotland, though it did erode part of the Calvinist base with the accelerating democratization of the American frontier. The third wave, Pentecostalism, reached still lower social levels, and did so in cultures relatively untouched by the other two, again with the exception of America. All three are religions of the word, achieving social mobility through education and mutual help, but only the first is associated with a developed 'high culture' of the word. There is no Methodist Milton or David Hume. None of them achieves an important musical culture, except in the form of democratic church song: the Calvinist metric psalm, the Methodist hymn, the Pentecostal chorus. The varying symbiosis between them is important. Not only does Methodism not expand where the Calvinist state churches have been successful, it is largely restricted to the Anglo-Saxon ambience. But in the areas of Methodist success Pentecostalism is relatively muted. Pentecostalism expands in places where Methodism and Calvinism rarely penetrated: the Catholic societies of Latin Europe and Latin America, the areas dominated by Lutheran state churches. In other words it expands now where the unitary principle allowed little room in earlier times for dissenting expansion. Here it is the dominant and most rapidly developing form of dissent but it comes too late and too low in the social scale to inhibit the development of class polarization in the manner achieved by Calvinism and Methodism, or to be the crucial factor in economic development represented by Calvinism.

Thus in Lutheran cultures explicit dissent tends to be late in arriving and to acquire a strong Pentecostal component. However, Lutheranism implies a development of the voluntaristic, lay, democratic principle *within* the Church itself, notably the Inner Mission. The Collegia Pietatis, the Moravian movement, the Inner Mission, the Haugean movement and its successors represented cells of personal, lay, incipiently democratic and pluralistic development within the Lutheran Church. In Anglicanism such movements developed into separatism during the course of the seventeenth and eighteenth centuries; in Lutheranism they did not. In various parts of Scandinavia they linked not only with democratization but with local cultural defence, notably in south and west Norway, where they were bastions of Norwegian national awareness. Thus they became linked to a periphery posed against a centre as well as a secondary élite posed against a primary one: in that they are precisely parallel to the position of Methodism in Wales. There are also some parallels with fundamentalism viewed as the cultural defence of rural, small-town America. Naturally, the role of cultural defence or guardian of national awareness inhibits the degree of pure voluntarism which can be instituted.

Let me summarize what I have suggested so far. Christianity initiates successive waves of pluralism because it is based on a *double entendre*: the Kingdom of God set over against principalities and powers. Nevertheless the dialectic of the Kingdom *reflects* the principalities and powers even as it subverts them. The dialectic gradually succumbs to a unitary pull which achieves its apogee in the baroque nation state. The nation state rejects the two realms of medieval civilization and provides a variety of moulds for the next wave of the counter-culture dialectic: Protestant dissent. Where it is least successful the dialectic is driven down to the level of psychological motifs; where it is most successful the knot of state and Church is completely untied and universal dissent becomes itself 'established', as in America. There are intermediate situations to be found in Britain and Scandinavia. Protestant dissent itself comes in three waves, the Calvinist, the Methodist and the Pentecostal, corresponding to successive waves of democratization.

In the contemporary world both the feudal dialectic of the two swords and of Protestant dissent have partially lapsed, and the unitary pull of social homogeneity has re-established itself. Far from being pluralistic, modern society is much less so than in the heyday of dissenting religion. Just as kings fought for the sacral unity of their realms against monk and pope, just as the baroque state endeavoured to eliminate incipient dissent, so contemporary society has produced its own unitary religion, which is compound of civic virtue and what is labelled folk-religiosity. This is a religion of habit and the *status quo*, devoted not to choice but to the community of generation, in particular the family since this is now the locus of cultural inertias and the stronghold of 'the given'. However, against this has arisen a third counter-culture, surfacing most dramatically in the student movement but corresponding to that 'free', mutable symbolization of the axes of human experience described by Robert Bellah. It is now appropriate to describe the character of contemporary folk-religiosity and to indicate the way in which the new counter-culture struggles both against the powers of the community of generation *and* against the previous manifesta-tions of the dialectic, especially the Protestant ethic. It will be argued that this latest counter-culture is the most evanescent of manifestations of the dialectic, because more socio-logically unrealistic than either of its two predecessors.

The dominant religion of the western world partakes of the general character of the society to which it belongs: it is non-participant, non-observant. It communicates via radio and television to an uncritical mass, but the Mass itself attracts few communicants. People attend with a certain occasional conformity civic and familial rituals, but the Church finds it difficult to be the active centre of a regular community. It is relatively successful in the urban villas with the privatized style of those areas, but distinctly unsuccessful with the male, the post-adolescent, and the worker and the inhabitant of the vast impersonal housing complex. There is a majority who believe in God, a certain public respect for Him and His advocates, but the activities associated with His Name are regarded as simply boring or incomprehensible. There is a widespread invocation of luck or fate, less so of Providence, and some vague hopes are cherished concerning death. Positive devotion is not admired, apart from family prayers, and to be 'religious' is to be somewhat odd. Meanwhile, each sphere of life has been largely released from religious conceptualization and ecclesiastical influence: political ideology, education, economy and welfare. The Church itself achieves a partial autonomy from the state, developing a critical attitude in its specialized agencies some-what distinct from the politics of goodwill which dominate its suburban constituencies.

This vague, unformulated, inarticulate faith is civic religion in so far as it pertains to the continuities of the community of generation; that is, to that which ought to be passed on. It is Durkheimian in that it relates to social order. Thus Christianity is believed to be a code which ensures minimum social decencies. That such a view should predominate in Lutheran societies is, of course, a peculiar irony. The emphasis on order implies that what is performed rests for justification on the fact that it has been done before and because it relates to the unit of generation, the family. Baptisms, marriages, funerals and (in Scandinavia) confirmation are sacred points of intersection in the familial cycle: people cannot explain their participation outside the notion of customary procedure. Perhaps they never could. There is a very strong desire that children should receive religious instruction and be initiated into the basic rites on the part of the people who remember nothing of that instruction except that they were glad they received it, who see no obligations deriving from the rites, and who hope the state will pass on what they do not feel able or willing to communicate themselves. If one adds to this a belief that nature and life are the proper sources of the religious sense and not confrontation with a divine Word of a personal Saviour, then it is clear that one has a form of natural, legalistic religion which is not a demand but a habit, not a choice but an inheritance. Explicit Christian commitment belongs to minority, to a counter-culture: perhaps it always did.

It is often said that we have a plural and rationalized society, but that depends on what is meant. Certainly the options are officially open; and the technical procedures are rational in a limited sense. In fact the religion is *not* plural but astonishingly unitary not only within cultures but across them, from Greater Copenhagen to Greater London and Greater Melbourne. It has little to do with rationality or enlightenment or science and everthing to do with norms of limited reciprocity, civic decencies, rites of public and private passage.

In a sense it is secular in the special sense of secular here employed: the Durkheimian identity of religion and society, the perennial secularization to which religion is perpetually subject. It relates most closely to a secular religion: Ancient Judaism.[3] Perform the rites, remember the pit from which your fathers were dug, keep the rules. Baptism serves as a Christian circumcision: the badge of entry into the community of generation. In Sweden the proportion of those marrying in church rose, a natural enough development showing proper respect for the unit of generation.

No doubt Jews imagine they are a minority, but they are only such in that they belong to a Durkheimian religion which has been excluded by those very Durkheimian forces which Judaism exemplifies – a description which today one may claim by mere existence in an ethnic category. Durkheim was, after all, a spoilt rabbi, and constructed from his experience the relation of religion to social identity and unity. Of course, underneath the rules and codes lies the hedonistic undertow of paganisms and superstition. Whether the resulting amalgam is correctly described as Ancient Judaism or not it certainly has a rather partial overlap with the religion of Augustine, Luther, Pascal, Blake and Kierkegaard. What this situation does to the evolutionary schemata we propose to describe for religious development, I cannot imagine.

What counter-culture can the dialectic generate against this normative consensus; what attack is possible on this passive but resistant centre? From Stockholm to New York there is (*was*, rather), the student movement, which is religious without institutionalization, or dogmatic coherence. It lacks institutionalization and coherence because it recognizes that each assault on the centripetal forces of society has had to sustain itself by recourse to similar forces. Thus it aspires to locate itself outside social time and space: to be literally extempore. It plays with many Christian motifs in an extempore fashion but desires no continuity with the past because everything is to be made new. Like the Protestant lay movements of the past it devises extempore rituals, open-air meetings, but these must never become a form. They have one object: to illustrate the capacity to devise, invent, create, illustrate freedom. Repeat the illustration and freedom is disproved. The only thing that can be repeated is the basic fact of disorganization itself. A sprawl of hippies provides its paradigm – and with a nice sense of irony the most prominent sprawl of hippies in Stockholm has established itself on the terrace of the Göteborg Bank.

The motifs are familiar and I only want to point to certain

elements of interest for this particular thesis. The first is that they repeat the Christian dialectic of a thrust above and below the established community. The second is that they take certain themes like choice, the condition of being childlike and the need for feminization, pushing each to its furthest logical limit. The third simply consists of a re-emphasis on the fact that they illustrate very strongly the dialectic *between* major counter-cultures as well perhaps as a dialectic within them. Not only is the major thrust of our current counter-culture against the Protestant ethic, but it also attacks the contemporary analogue of monkishness: the academic. And just as monasticism repeated its protest in a series of waves and Protestant dissent similarly, so the student movement comes in waves. The difference is that the monastic waves were long and slow, the waves of Protestant dissent relatively rapid but distinguishable, whereas the waves of current protest overlap in a completely confused succession. Its intermittent, evanescent character is part of its logic.

The thrust above and below established society is clear enough. Contemporary revolt aspires to build a local commune and a universal community: this means it is both monastic and catholic, but it abhors the state. Both commune and community are composed of these born originally in the contiguities of place, nation and family but who have been born again with similar souls. The phrase 'born again' links not only with Protestant dissent but also with its opposite because 'born again' means desocialization *per se*, not resocialization. In order to resocialize against the community, against its natural thoughtless relaxation and convivial pull, Protestant dissent rejected alcohol, whereas in order to desocialize totally the current protest welcomes drugs. It desires the undifferentiated world of a newly born being, before norms, before categories, before control even of functions. This links with two other motifs: feminization and voluntarism. Sexual differentiation is, of course, an aspect of categorization and normative control, but the specifically male component in that differentiation has emphasized discipline and the military virtues. Hence the shift towards undifferentiated humanity must also include a rejection of that male component. The long process of feminization through the Marian devotion and the Christmas feast and through the psychology underpinning the peace movements reaches here its conclusion. It does so just as the assertion of the voluntary principle also reaches *its* fullest point. The monks created a community of choice by some of the most rigorous resocialization procedures ever devised. Current protest invents *de*socialization procedures, on the assumption that choice is a natural human attribute preceding society. The monks and Protestants resocialized against natural sin; contemporary protest desocializes back to inherent perfection. Thus it plunges back into Nature and its God is the great soul of immanence. Once again an ancient level of religious feeling is re-tapped and our evolutionary schemata of religious development are shaken. At this juncture of course the Christian motifs become merged in those of eastern religion. Total freedom includes the likelihood of eclecticism and eastern motifs are not compromised by association with western civic power. However, eastern religion saw even the attainment of unity with the All as the faintly possible conclusion of the most exacting resocialization, whereas for contemporary radical religiosity it must be instant and immediate. The Christian notion that all may be saved has crossed with the eastern concept of pantheistic union and with the notion of the natural pre-social goodness of man to produce the idea that all men may be mystics provided they reject society and socialization.

One final link is notable. The established community is rooted in the body, in the biological continuities of generation, and it uses the analogies of the body: it is the body politic, the citizen body. The monks broke their links with biological pressures and with the body politic to belong to the body of Christ, to live and feed on the heavenly food and be wedded to the heavenly bridegroom. Both the biological and the civic are a corpus of rules against which monk and dissenter set higher rules. It was an affirmation of choice made at the cost of the human and the social body. But contemporary revolt attempts to rise above the rules by rejecting *all* rules, and therefore returns to man's pre-social biological condition, i.e. to a determined sphere of nature. This is its basic contradiction and its discontinuity with the Christian counter-cultures of the past. With the use of drugs the assertion of ecstasy becomes itself mechanistic.

My theme has been the creation of counter-cultures based on choice set against the community of generation. As I have already suggested, the monks chose the holy community, the Protestants chose a relationship with a holy person, the contemporary radicals sanctify the notion of choice itself. The three with which I have been concerned have represented different types of margin fighting the centre with different advantages and disadvantages. The monks often retired to a geographical margin and there showed they understood the paradox that choice depends on resocialization. But they could only be an isolated witness to a principle they were unable to generalize. The early Protestants were another type of margin, constituting in their original thrust a secondary élite struggling to innovate against the power of rigid centres and concerned to generalize the principle of commitment and choice. They neither saw that their protest would become the basis of established Protestant state churches nor that to the extent personal choice was accepted, it undermined their own chance of survival. They went further than the monks and encountered a deeper recalcitrance. The students today are a disappointed élite, forming a movement at the centre against the very concept of a centre, personal or communal or normative. They have no standards either in the sense of rules or national flags. This is the furthest limit of attack on the centre and the most unrealistic and uncreative in its strategy. To attack the community of generation so totally is to destroy one's own base, and to become, as Luther sadly said of the Reformation, *res unius aetatis*, a thing of one generation. A religion of the fathers – Abraham,

Isaac, Jacob – has tremendous powers of survival and runs from generation to generation; a religion composed solely of sons is by definition and social logic *res unius aetatis*.

Notes

1. I should emphasize that I am *not* attempting any variety of the philosophy of history. I am indicating the social logic and varied opportunity costs of three different *types* of assertion of the notion of choice. Since this analysis is ideal-typical in the Weberian sense I do not feel the need to enter into the actual historical variety of monasticism.

2. Of course, this links with counter-cultural motifs in Judaism. Judaism is in one sense Durkheimian but the suffering servant is a *collective* embodiment of power realized in weakness and rejection which complements the *individual* embodiment in Christ. This is why the profoundest elements in Christianity rest so explicitly on Deutero-Isaiah. Islam largely lacks this Judaeo-Christian ambiguity so that even its sanctity tends to be transmitted by naturalistic lineages, and the notion of redemption by suffering is highly uncongenial to it as compared with male ideals of victory in holy war.

3. I am particularly grateful to Dr. Per Salomonsen for suggesting this point about Judaism and for his analysis of contemporary natural religion published in *Religion i Dag*, V. E. Gad, Copenhagen, 1971. I may add that the rise in church marriages which took place in Sweden in the 1960s and which I refer to on page 14 was not maintained.

II

Traditional Religion and the Traditional Transitions to the Tradition of the New

I am a traditionalist; and I am an exponent of one of the most modern forms of self-consciousness, sociology. Tradition is concerned with what is given, and sociology is concerned with givens, data. Tradition is the social *a priori*, what is taken for granted so that it is hardly recognized as taken for granted. Sociology takes nothing for granted, except the existence of contingent regularities, relations and conditions. So a sociologist who is a traditionalist is going either to be a very schizoid character; or he is going to be a quirky, off-beat traditionalist. At the very least he will be self-conscious about his traditionalism, and self-conscious tradition is already not quite pure traditionality. A traditional society spawns neither sociologists nor traditionalists: only a society where tradition is under threat will produce traditionalists and sociologists. A sociologist is necessarily a person whose roots have been disturbed enough to ask questions of the ground of his being; a self-conscious traditionalist is likely to be a person who defends tradition on grounds which are wider than the mere existence of traditional modes. He will be anxious to show that some roots are necessary to man's well-being, that some accepted ground makes creative variation possible. In short he will argue that the aims of modern man will be better served if he recognizes the role of tradition and understands its value for human beings. The truly traditional person does not justify tradition on such grounds. I do.

So traditionalism and traditionality are rather different things. Yet the question remains: how and why do we recommend tradition in the modern situation?

It depends what you mean by tradition. Since the context is traditional religion I can set aside areas of interest indicated by phrases like 'the democratic tradition' or 'the revolutionary tradition', 'the Ibo tradition', 'the university tradition'. I do not have to deal with all these varied forms and varied meanings of tradition, but only with traditional religion as understood by people with a Jewish or Christian background. That limits my interest but still does not focus it. I still have to define what I mean by traditional religion in that limited sector of concern. I can do it either by pointing to a particular religion (or to a group of religions) which it seems reasonable to call 'traditional'. Or I can pick out a particular element in religion which I call 'traditional'. The choice is far from easy. If you think of Judaism it may seem odd to label it *tout court* as *a* traditional religion. Judaism contains different traditions which make varied attempts to encompass modernity. It is easy to suggest that only orthodox Judaism is traditional Judaism, by which one means that it has been there longer than the other forms. But I do not want to base my discussion on a definition which restricts me to the oldest strands of religion. Age in itself provides no substantive sociological or theological category. It is also possible to suggest that it is the very fact of religion itself that constitutes tradition. All religion in the modern world is marked by traditionality. No matter how trendy, hip or semi-secular, provided the phenomenon is definable as religion by some criterion or other then it is *ipso facto* traditional.

Of course here begins the usual dizzying regress or progress of definitions which I cut short by defining my concern as the traditional elements in the kind of religion which we know as native speakers of the language of Christianity or Judaism. What those traditional elements are will be indicated by the range of questions which I now attempt to cover. I intend to be a genuine instance of tradition in one respect: I do not define tradition, I exemplify it. And my first act of exemplification will be to take examples from my own tradition. Tradition knows no better than its own. I start where I am.

Tradition knows no better than its own. The phrase is ambiguous: it means either that there is no recognition of what lies outside or it means that recognition is combined with secure knowledge of superiority. So the first question that modernity poses for tradition is one of belonging and the second question is one of the right evaluation of belonging. How is it possible to belong? How does one relate belonging to other alien forms of adherence? How shall we still say 'all the gods of the heathen are as idols but the Lord made the heavens'? As Zwi Werblowsky has pointed out: every universal religion must have a doctrine of other religions.[1]

I begin with my first question: what is involved in belonging, in adhering to a tradition? Tradition is based on a single universe of meaning. Once fracture that universe and its internal harmonies are lost for ever. This is essentially what is meant by pluralism. The traditional man dwelt under a sacred canopy that defined the limits of meaning and foreclosed on the possibility of alternatives. This can lead either to tolerance or gross *in*tolerance. Total security within an unquestioned world makes it easy to relax. You do not ask questions about the boundaries when these are co-extensive with the furthest horizon, unless you elect to travel, in which case you do. If you elect to travel then you must either *be* the elect or simply yield your world up to others. So the enclosed, unexpanded universe of tradition has to come in two forms: as the given, unquestioned *a priori* of all experience, or as the chosen, elected *a priori*. It must either be the total categorical apparatus of knowing and being, so intimate as to be past noticing, or it is the self-consciously chosen assumption. Once chosen that assumption must by an inherent social and sociological obligation realize its implications. Not to choose is to live securely within what is, prior even to recognition of the condition in which you live, move and have your being. To choose is to be committed to a train of consequences as incalculable as they are inevitable. There is an important sense in which Judaism is the first non-traditional religion. Abraham was called and was thereby elect; he went out not knowing whither he went. He was the prototype of the Pilgrim, going out to a city and a land which the Lord should give him. The Puritan and the Jew share a common paradigm, in which choice and election are central and in which they together inexorably demand commitment to what lies over the horizon.

The social *a priori*, chosen as an assumption and not accepted automatically as the frame of being, has to devise protective clauses. An expedition across frontiers requires an apparatus of protective and explicit rules. The existentially chosen requires explicit law. Choice means codification. If you do not encode your choice it will simply cease to operate as a continuing option. The expedition which has no rules simply cannot keep itself going. The very idea of the chosen *a priori*, the existentially selected assumption, cannot survive without reliance on a sense of the unequivocally given.

What is above all unequivocal is 'the Call'. Once there is an unequivocal call there must be separation. You must be called *out*. So the logic of choice involves both the rule book and segregation, and thereby rules of segregation. The break with the automatically given must restore part of the automatically given to survive. This is the underlying economy of society: to achieve change you must make heavy concessions to the *status quo*. Above all, one element of the *status quo* is absolutely essential to the maintenance of the impetus of change and that is a sense of the very existence of a *status quo*. An explicit doctrine of impetus must be embedded beyond question in the very structure of social perceptions and the individual psyche. No counter without culture, no pilgrim without a law and a book, no travel without an untouchable Ark, no existential trust without a binding agreement. Change rests on the given; choice depends on the bond which binds.

So election means covenant and the idea of religion alters its meaning. One interpretation of 'religio' rests on the notion of binding. But the binding has changed its character. Tradition was first the categorical apparatus by which the horizons of men in this society and in that were defined. They were bound by that obligatory frame. Then the tradition became a new bond, based on calling. The calling was a bond: the rule-book, the explicit way, the exchange of a word. A bond is based on the giving of a word. And the word *came*: it was given and accepted as given. To put it in this way is not primarily to describe a historical process whereby an Israel or a new Israel came into being and bound itself together with a binding book of bonds and promises. It is to indicate a social logic: the chosen is the explicit and the bounded.

There are limits to choice, and different breaks with traditions encounter different limits. That point can be re-phrased as follows: each different type of break with tradition breeds a specific traditionality. The challenge of that dawning modernity which constituted the encounter of Abraham with a Covenant God opened up a specific kind of historical movement and a specific kind of counter-movement. The New Israel of the Christian Church carried in it the seed of a social logic which must encase and enclose it. Each experiment exists under certain highly limiting conditions. We can say that Judaism is a revelation of one kind and Christianity a revelation of another, and that they exist in a continuum of time. But they also exist as alternative social logics, distinct and overlapping, and they encounter different costs and limits. They both contain the idea of the revealed, which refers to what is uncovered. That is an overlap in the two experiments. They both must embody the pre-conditions under which the experiment – any experiment – can be successfuly maintained. That is another point of overlap. But equally they embody alternative social logics, operating outside those overlaps. Both kinds of anti-traditionalism must be expressed in defined specific, different traditions. And the closer the overlap and genetic contiguity the stronger must be the protective casings and protecting clauses. In short both religions are committed to belonging and to a doctrine of the nature of the connection between them. The first must see the second as a deviation and the second must see the first as an antecedent preparation. Such interpretations must in turn accelerate the spirals of mutual repulsion set in being by the entrenched protecting clauses. Trenches must be dug wherever a small no-man's-land divides. Mutually adjacent experiments exist in conditions which govern their coexistence. Not only is there a social logic which governs the initial choice, but there is a social logic which governs the mutual relation of choices which grow genetically out of each other and which lie contiguously on a continuum of types of choice. The entrenchment demanded by choice is deepened by the contiguity of choices. Close relationship creates repulsion and an incest taboo.

So we have come full circle to where I began: secure belonging and the estimate and ranking of alternative forms of belonging. Christianity and Judaism were initially breaks in those great chains of social being which bound everyone down to a single horizon. They began to move and initiated the idea of *a* movement and the movement of history. They had to have a law of their own members, and to link that law with the law of the one universe as ruled by the one God. They were bound not only with a bond of election but were also bound in the sense of having direction. Pilgrim was bound towards a City. But these breaks encounter modern conditions which make problematic the continuity of previous breaks. What is new about the modern breaking of tradition is that it threatens the previous breakages. Of course, Christianity threatened Judaism, but it did not institute a set of general conditions which made the continuity of Judaism inherently hazardous. Indeed, the external threat was an assistance to the process of drawing boundaries and making protective entrenchments deeper. Modernity, by virtue of plurality and mobility, threatens the very possibility of entrenchment. Previous challenges created entrenchment; the modern challenge threatens entrenchment.

This is a very special kind of threat because it means that the modern experiment, if it can be called that, destroys the previous experiments which prepared the way. Both the idea of a chosen, choosing man and of a chosen, choosing people contained the seed of modern mobility. They were ideas about movement. They were social movements. And what threatens those movements is precisely mobility. It is often said that Christianity is its own grave digger, but that capacity to threaten itself is most paradoxically illustrated in the fate that befalls the idea of movement. We must look at that fate more carefully because you will already have picked up an ambiguous overtone in the word 'movement'. I began by latching on to an ambiguous overtone inside the phrase 'tradition knows no better'. The ambiguity inside the word movement is much more crucial to my argument. Modernity is movement, both a total mobility and a total commitment. The logic of choice has either shifted into total openness, or it has shifted towards total closure. People move, people join movements.

The old traditional forms of anti-tradition were Judaism and Christianity and they embodied God's people, Israel, and the people of God, the 'New Israel'. They also embodied man directly face to face with God. The movement and the breakage were collective *and* individual and the two were in creative tension. The collective englobed the individual, simultaneously constricting and protecting him. The individual rested on the base which tradition provided to criticize tradition and to proclaim his freedom within it. Jewish prophetism and Christian martyrdom belong to that essential tradition. Judaism and Christianity were traditions of the break which provided bases for breaks in tradition under certain limiting and limited conditions. But what seems to be happening now is a bifurcation of the idea of movement. One arm of the bifurcation is based on total individual mobility, at least as an ideal if not as an achieved reality. The other arm of the bifurcation is based on collective movement and a movement towards collectivism. The new mobility destroys old belongings and the entrenched clauses ranking and evaluating alternative belongings. The new collectivism destroys all antecedent collectivities, typically of course through the demands of the party or the state, and above all in the coalescence of party and state. Modernity either wrecks belonging or re-establishes it in a more total manner. Perhaps there is even an analogy here with what Judaism and Christianity did *vis-à-vis* mere traditionality. Because they embodied choices and destinations they demanded more explicit and complete loyalties. The modern movements towards liberation and historic destiny demand even more complete and avowed loyalties. They only allow prophets *for* them and martyrs *for* them; they do not envisage prophets and martyrs against them. The relationship between the demands of traditional religions like Judaism and Christianity and these new demands must be explored below.

How do the two old experiments, related as they are in historic tension and mutual exclusion, confront modernity in its two mutually exclusive forms: as total mobility and as total mobilization? To answer that question we must first examine the difference between the two original experiments.

This is not an exercise in comparative religion so much as a delineation of contiguous and overlapping logics to which may be assigned the preliminary identification discs of 'Judaism' and 'Christianity'. I am writing in terms of ideal types, and the validity of my sociological observations on these alternative types of breakage and of tradition is quite separate from any question as to the ontological validity of the religions themselves.

An unequivocal call creates particularity. The basic myths of Israel and of the Church relate to a call. Come ye out. . . . Follow me. A call is a demand, a mission and a name. The particular nation and the particular man were given a name which established peculiarity and uniqueness. The logic of Judaism is that of a people and a mission, and the logic of Christianity is that of a man and a mission. Hence arise the varied stresses within the two religions on individuality and commonality respectively. The singular man, first person singular plays a relatively greater part in Christianity than the singular people. This is not to say, of course, that the idea of the pilgrim people, the 'people of God' is not very important in Christianity.

The call is to achieve universality by way of particularity, and it thereby introduces an anticipatory element and the idea of the proleptic event. Both Judaism and Christianity are movements of history and movements of people, and the anticipation written in the foundation documents of each sees the fact of choice – choosing and chosen – as the first movement in a universal liberation. So here we have the basic ground or pattern of all modern mass movements: the movement of history, the destiny of a particular category or vanguard, and the extension of the particular to the universal at a given point in the future. If you add to these basic characteristics the sociological aspects I mentioned earlier, such as a rule-book, carefully protected boundaries, entrenched clauses constantly reiterated, bonds – you have almost all the features of modern messianism. The historic shape of the mass movement is discernible in Judaism and in Christianity. It is the latent model, printed like a paradigm at the level of the subconscious, waiting to be activated by structural openings.

Yet there are differences as important as the overlap. Judaism stresses a people in a *place*. Since a people in a place must be genetically defined it also stresses elements of familial continuity. It deals with a succession of family patriarchs. The choice *of* a people and choice *by* a people necessarily restricts emphasis on individual choice in the person. So the stress on the collectivity will lead to a further emphasis on what is exterior and binding: the rule and the law. Law will be the basic principle and with law – justice.

A place, a people and a law. There is an exteriority binding all into one, and expressed in ritual. Ritual is the protective casing, the necessary support system underlying law; and it simultaneously wards off intrusive elements. Ritual not only regulates but provides definition. Your control system is simultaneously your boundary marker. And where this can be done by principles of conduct and distinctive modes of *behaviour* it does not need to be done by explicit doctrinal formulae. A people, a collective, which constitute an ethnic and/or cultural unity can be marked off by what is done rather than what is believed.

This leads to a distinction which is perhaps *the* crucial distinction. Christianity shifts the focus off a concrete people, a place, and a defined, imposed regulation, to a chosen belief. That belief is not assent to a proposition but interior response. So the criteria of aceptability shifts from automatic member-ship and from obedience to a regulative principle, to a quality of subjective relation. Now it is quite obvious that this shift towards individuality, towards a choice exercised within the individual life cycle, and towards an interior relation or response, occurs mainly at the level of symbols and paradigms. Important shifts occur when the new paradigms are proclaimed at the point of origination, but the regulative, group principles and boundary markers have to be re-admitted in order to maintain the revised paradigm in being. Enormous psychic and social resources have to be directed and diverted to the task of maintenance. Indeed, in so far as the new paradigm strains against the natural conditions of group maintenance much has to be conceded to those conditions. The more you go against sociological nature the more you must concede to it. A special disposition of the maintenance system is necessary to secure the survival of what cannot be relied on to occur naturally. Judaism relies on natural mechanisms which it reinforces; Christianity has to reinforce itself with mechanisms designed to counteract the pull of nature. Yet the crucial transition to a new interior paradigm has been made and it is radical enough to be sociologically unrealistic. The choosing man, rooted in a qualitative internal act, cast in the mould of an individual redemptive example, is possible as an ideal but very problematic as a reality and positively misleading as social description. The individualistic paradigm requires heavy collective casing,

expressed above all in the monastic order; and it also requires a
guerrilla war against ordinary natural processes, and that war is
expressed in the monastic discipline and the Puritan character
structure. The mutation towards interiority is so dangerous and
the protective casings have to be so heavily reinforced that the
long-term movement is littered by fossilization and blind alleys.
Only one or two exemplars of the paradigm are going to slide
around or under the net of sociological rules. Yet slide under the
net they do, and they are assisted by an odd conjunction with
helpful developments in the collectivist variant of the logic of
choice. I mean that the evolution of Christianity is eventually
affected by the evolution of Judaism and of the Jews, especially
since the Enlightenment.

Because the collective variant is necessarily particular it
constitutes a minority devising heavy protective devices against
the majority. The spiral of mutual repulsions described earlier
then builds up structures of resentment so that whenever
ordinary social processes corrode the casing, the individuals
released into the general concourse of society at large are likely
to join the corrosive elements eating at the regulative principles
of the majority. They will embrace extreme individualistic
principles, outdistancing the individualism of the majority, or
they will search for a radical counter-collective outdistancing
even the group controls operated by the minority. The minority
once broken up then becomes part of a vanguard carrying
forward the ideals which were previously more characteristic of
the majority. And because those principles are inherently as
dangerous to overall social coherence and to any particular
social order as the existence of extensive minorities, the pressure
of majority against minority grows, with mutual extremisms
undergoing simultaneous accelerations. Thus developments
which assist the ultimate breakthrough to interiority must be
marked by very intense activity of counter-mechanisms and
accelerated processes of division affecting and attacking minority
cells floating in the wider body. The breakdown of the initial
protective casing around the minority breeds even more divisive

criteria of distinctiveness and repulsion. In saying this I am partly stating some general dynamic properties of majority-minority relationships and partly pointing to some additional accelerators based on such factors as genetic contiguity and the special protecting devices required to maintain mutations in active or in fossilized form. I am trying to suggest why the most violent pressure will develop against the minority when the ghetto casing is corroded.

Such then are the relations which do exist and from time to time are likely to exist between the contiguous alternative expressions of the logic of choice. Now we must examine what happens to the individual interior variant and to the collective external variant under the conditions of the peculiarly modern individualism and the peculiarly modern collectivism. In short what happens to Judaism and Christianity faced by individualistic mobility and by totalitarian, collective mobilization? I have already touched on one aspect of this as part of the tension between Judaism and Christianity and I do not need to reformulate it under the head of a reaction to modernity. The corrosion of Judaism, assisting the corrosion of Christianity, is simultaneously part of the dynamics of their mutual relationship *and* part of the dynamics of their confrontation with modernity. I need only repeat that those set floating away from their moorings in the historically over-pressured minority will move towards extreme interiority and extreme collectivism. And perhaps one might add that the dynamics of the majority reaction to this and to its own internal dissolutions will lead to collectivist manifestations, e.g. Nazism, capable of generating very general reactions against all collective constraints. I mean that Christendom can breed collectivist mobilizations which then arouse very widespread reactions against every form of legitimate authority and against every limit, even the limits imposed by reason. But that is to anticipate and it introduces illustrations drawn from very recent history indeed. I want now to return to the internal development of the majority system, i.e. Christianity, as it faces incipient and then mature modernity.

Modernity introduces cumulative fragmentations at the level of communal organization which induce tendencies towards extreme manifestations of interiority and extreme variants of collectivism. The model for the collectivism and for associated mass movements has already been described and it is taken over with only minor modifications. Many such takeovers are secular, but others are based on the idea of a pilgrim people, either acting redemptively for the world as in the case of the U.S.A. or beleaguered by the forces of darkness as in South Africa. The model for interiority is mediated by Christianity as such and then made available by specific modifications which attempt to keep individuality under control. Christianity has to control its own potentialities if they are not to explode. Methodism is precisely such a modification, controlling interiority in a collective frame. It thereby provides an example of how the latent interiority of Christianity is released and an example of a mass movement exercising realistic but not over-determined collective controls. This enables Methodism to be utilized as a bridge passage to modernity, carrying interiority without anarchy and constituting a movement of the mass without collective terror and totalitarian bonding. The Jewish analogue of Methodism, which I take to be eighteenth-century Hassidism, has to develop somewhat differently. Hassidism operates in too small and undifferentiated a context to consti-tute a full-blown semi-modern compromise and tends to fall back therefore on a mystical interiority posed against – and protected by – the orthodox collective.

Movements like Methodism have continued from the onset of modern industrialism until now and they have controlled both the ravages of anomie, and the extreme manifestations of interiority. They have stood between the individual and the state and have lain sufficiently in the path of radical social movements to temper their acerbity and their will to create total environments. In short Methodism and similar movements have characterized situations of social and political pluralism without collapsing into pure interiority and fragmentation. However, they have only been able to do this in Protestant societies. Catholic societies under the pressure of modernity have experienced an initial tightening of the collectivist principle in religion, first after Trent and especially after 1870; and they have stimulated radical movements based on the same collectivist model. The latent interiority of Catholicism has only been released since 1960 and has since then proved fairly destructive. Catholicism could not and did not spawn the Methodist transition; it first tightened its internal control and then tried to create its own variant on interiority.

I am not of course attempting to discuss the shifts of the modern period purely in terms of the initial logic of a religion. I am saying that certain models are imprinted and are released under congruent social circumstances, tempering or accelerating the tendencies derived from the direct logic of the situation. A latent model of interiority will normally be controlled strictly within a collective framework. It may be partly released in some religious modification such as Methodism and then escape into culture at large where it joins with all kinds of secular variants. By the time that has happened nobody can tell where the complex channels of influence lie. I am not even interested in attempting to chart such obscurities. Nor will I try to assess what derives from the direct logic of modern situations and what shapings, modifications, temperings, or even accelerations are received from antecedent religious forms. I am interested in the problem stated at the beginning: belonging and a secure evaluation of that belonging. The challenge of modernity to our belonging is posed by fragmentations which induce pure interiority and reactions of an extreme collectivist kind. The classic dilemma of sociology is correctly stated: how are the cultures intermediate between the naked individual and the impersonal grid of the bureaucratic state to be maintained?

The problem of pure interiority derives from the fragmenting potential of modern social structures and is shaped and informed by the latent interiority carried by Christianity. I intend no more than the briefest statement of that problem.

Judaism and Catholic Christianity have both controlled the logic of choice within a vigorous collective bond. They have switched the focus back to behavioural criteria specified in terms of externalities and have defined membership not so much by choice as by genetic or quasi-genetic inheritance. But once membership or belonging is focused on choice and on states of genuine inwardness a corrosive logic is set in motion which extends indiscriminately to every sector of activity. All structures of convenience, and all hierarchies of achievement are undermined by the appeal to inwardness and choice. Settled points of transition, conventions of discourse, specified modalities of language, structured cues as to behaviour, rules governing the interlocking of statuses – all these are unhinged by the appeal to inwardness and feeling. By the same token the external assessment of competence, capacity and achievement is undercut by the single criterion: genuine/non-genuine.

It is this logic, initiated at the margin by Israel and accelerated by Christianity, especially by Protestant Christianity, which illustrates most dramatically the potential of an idea to destroy the base from which it began. That destruction is not merely a matter of the historical base but includes the sociological base. The trend to interiority, bereft of specific content, of hierarchical competence, of ritual sequence and of specified limitations corrodes not only society but self. The challenge of modernity is to create structures of belonging at least strong enough to prevent the logic of choice destroying even the self. Traditional religion has performed this task by criteria of external behaviour or automatic membership as well as by the careful elaboration of sequences, respects, modalities and transitions. It has controlled by respect and by rite rather than by individual incentive or by collective terror. The challenge of modernity is to use those traditional resources to limit the ravages of spontaneity on the one hand and of pure collective terror on the other.

Perhaps I should add a concluding postscript setting the above argument in the context of secularization. Traditional religion has controlled secularity and the sacred by the very fact of their potent opposition and contrast. It has varied the boundaries and forms of the opposition but never eliminated it. The individual has been controlled in some degree within a collective framework and neither his personal wishes not his status have been accorded unequivocal sacredness. Even individualistic religion has retained a reference point 'beyond' the individual. Similarly, there has been no conferral of unequivocal sacredness on movements of the collective: even the Church is under 'judgement'. Thus both spontaneity and collective terror have been confronted with an inhibition.

The modern situation includes the possibility that the inhibition may be removed. Individuals may conceive themselves as the ultimate point of reference and may embody 'the father's will' without remainder. In Christian terms everyman is an incarnation but there is no father, i.e. no tradition of the Fathers, no father (or mother) superiors, no God the Father. This makes the individual desire of the moment absolute without qualification. It represents complete secularization and extends the doctrine of the incarnation to the point where it is destroyed by virtue of its universalization.

On the other side there is the collective movement of 'the people' ultimately victorious within history, crossing a new Jordan into a land of liberty and promise, qualitatively different from all the landscapes of the past. This too secularizes the Judaeo-Christian paradigm. History becomes the sole judge and an ultimate triumph is assured within historic time. The pilgrim people under God then become a universal 'People' and the one, holy, undivided pilgrim band becomes coextensive with the godhead. It may then do as it wills and treat its political imperatives as identical with the will of heaven. This secularization has been approached time and again in the past, especially where kings have ruled by divine right and claimed the power to heal men's diseases. The modern period has completed that ancient secularization, substituting only the tradition of divine peoplehood for divine kingship. It is therefore both apotheosis of religion and end of religion. The only tradition which can inhibit the tradition of secular divinities, collective or individual, is the tradition which maintains secular and sacred in a complex balance. Unless you have sacred *and* secular you cannot control the destructive potential of divinization.

Note

1. See Z. Werblowsky, *Beyond Tradition and Modernity*, Athlone Press, London, 1975.

III

Institutionalism and Community

To write an essay in synthesis on material provided by some thirty authors is to compose a very complicated kind of fugue. So complicated is the task that the present author can only hope that his readers will sympathize and recollect the double meaning of fugue: a flight of the intelligence and a flight from the intelligence, radical association and radical dissociation. A fugue consists of two elements: sections and themes. The sections can be simply stated. I shall begin with organizations which reflect in fairly direct manner modern society and what some regard as the defining character of modern society: bureaucracy. There follows next a consideration of the condition of the institutional church, afflicted both by the acids of modern society and the corrosions of various communitarian openings to the theological left. I shall then proceed to the old in the new and the new in the old, notably the varieties of modern pietism. Most of these have attracted another Weberian label: charismatic. Then I move to the subject of 'invisible religion', i.e. the survival of very ancient cultural pieties, the manifestations of civic cult, and the personal, variable poetry of the self-creating individual. Finally I shall indicate certain paradoxes in the modern situation.

So much for my basic sections; my themes are as follows: The underlying impulse of so many of the phenomena discussed by our thirty authors is a fear of institutionalization and a nostalgia for community. It is held that the individual is repressed by the segmented role-structure of institutions and realized by the pure, open, face-to-face humanity of communal living. The individual fears exteriority in the form of rationalized society, rationalized nature, or the otherness of God. He seeks to be out of the body, whether it is the body of Christ, the corpus of ecclesiastical dogma, the body of society or the limitation of his own corporeal existence. He rejects the Puritan character structure because it is a limit, a boundary and an organization of the psyche. He repudiates paternalism and the Almighty Father, because these represent the 'difficult' elements in society: authority, hierarchy and power. These, however, are only the subjects of the fugue; there are, as I shall argue, many counter-subjects.

The first of my sections is based on one of these counter-subjects, the influence and the frank acceptance of modern bureaucracy. The obvious examples are provided by such groups as Scientology and to a lesser extent Christian Science, but it is just as easy to illustrate the growth of administrative rationality and criteria of efficiency within the Church itself. *The* ministry has taken on many of the characteristics of *a* ministry. Not that this is entirely new: Henry VIII and Peter the Great both in different ways converted – if that is the right word – churches into nationalized industries. But such examples belong to a period when Church and administration were only marginally differentiated; the contemporary bureaucratization has occurred within a church largely separated off from general administration.

Movements like Scientology and Christian Science exemplify the ubiquity of bureaucracy in a different and more pervasive manner. They render social services rather than offering divine service. These social services are provided by experts who must receive appropriate certification in a body of gnosis conceived as analogous to or even superior to science. It is a question of imparting knowledge rather than eliciting faith. Knowledge requires exposition whereas faith inspires the expression of devotion. Like contemporary science knowledge flows authoritatively through organizational levels. Personal contact is largely between practitioner and client rather than within the multiple affective bonds of the worshipping community. The bureaucratic body protects its own integrity by carefully policing its own boundaries and defining the border between scientific truth and dangerous error. The cult, as Eister persuasively argues, is not necessarily so very loose in its structure. Furthermore, history is seen as the progressive winnowing of truth from error and it reaches a superior stage with the appearance of the new cult.

Clearly, whether exemplified in these modern cults or in the organization of churches bureaucratic tendencies are the reverse of those found in most of the phenomena under consideration. No doubt the outcry against bureaucracy and against segmental involvement is some index of the degree to which these things provide a pervasive environment to be fought against. But the churches show signs of the disembodied 'spirit' as well as of the encroachments of bureaucracy. This occurs in charismatic outbreaks, lay initiatives, translations of dogma into fluid symbolizations, prophetic criticisms of society, eschatological and mystical yearnings, communitarian groups of seekers anticipating the age of the spirit, the breakdown of all bounds between church and church, or church and humanity, and the corrosion of obedience to any coherent norms of conduct.

Perhaps the point at which to begin an analysis of the spirit and the churches is the breakdown of certainty, more particularly in the Roman Catholic Church. However, it could also be illustrated from the context of Jewry as discussed in the paper by Ben Simon on the French Jewish Community, or as recently researched in England. The Catholic and the Jewish cases differ of course. What they have in common is the breakdown of a sense of absolute, exterior ritual obligation. This allows an awareness of alternative loyalties to those provided by the quasi-biological continuities of the sacred society or the sacred ethnic group, whether these be ideological, pan-human or national loyalties. Both Catholic Church and Jewish community emerge from the ghetto and such terminology is peculiarly appropriate where Catholics have formed a well-drilled second column in a non-Catholic society. The very existence of high ghetto walls produces an integration which can explode outwards when the right mixture of elements is present. Holland is the obvious example of a tightly organized column of sheep who hear the voice of Rome so well that they actually tried to implement the aims of the Vatican Council. In a mobile society yet provided with ·strong lines of internal communication they were very susceptible to decentralization advocated from the centre. A similar disorientation occurred in American Catholicism, likewise regarded as being peculiarly loyal to the Roman obedience.

Associated with the loss of certainty has gone an increasing moral divergence. Of course, moral divergence is endemic, but in certain areas, more especially with regard to the norms governing the family, the Church had been able to exercise considerable influence. Yet it was precisely in these areas that its influence was relaxed. This occurred whether or not the institutional church flourished. In Poland and Ireland for example, countries where external repression had built up a union of national and religious identity and where church practice and sacerdotal recruitment are very strong, the divergence from official ethical norms is marked. The same is true of such a Catholic country as Spain even given the institutional revival of the 1940s and 1950s. Particularly amongst the young intelligentsia, but also more widely, the kind of teaching typified by Humanae Vitae or less controversially Catholic teaching on divorce and abortion, is disregarded.

In general, of course, formal institutional practice has weakened, sometimes quite recently as part of recent industrialization, sometimes as part of a very long tradition of institutional neglect, as in parts of S. Spain, SE. Italy, Montenegro and elsewhere. But in this sphere some paradoxes are immediately apparent. Institutional practice has often involved just that variety of popular Catholicism exemplified in Spain or in Brazil, or forms of superstition and manipulative magic even further removed from the classical norms of the Christian faith. This popular Catholicism could be described as privatized; it was certainly secularized in the special sense of being coextensive with cultural identity. To be Spanish was to be Catholic but equally to be *truly* Catholic was to be Spanish. Church and culture, Church and state were one. The new impulses given authority and direction by the Vatican Council restored the Bible and the Eucharist at the expense of peripheral and often manipulative devotional practices. Where Catholic practice is relatively low these reforms have had maximum impact so that the approach of the faithful is more specifically Catholic and based on a more personal faith than in areas of apparent Catholic dominance. Thus it is possible to argue that the Catholicism of northern Portugal is both more practised and less 'truly' Catholic than that of southern Portugal. Inevitably, one can dispute the significance of conformity to a more evangelical as distinct from a cultural or superstitious form of Catholicism.

A parallel tendency receiving accelerated expression through the agency of the Vatican Council involves a reformulation of the relationship between clergy and laity. There has, of course, been an almost universal difficulty in the recruitment of priests; Poland provides the one obvious exception. In some countries this is not a new trend. In Spain, for example, the ratio of priests to people has been dropping for a very long time and now drops again after a temporary halt in the mid-century. In Holland, by contrast, the crisis affects a country once noted for its eager aspirants to the priesthood.

The clergy are peculiarly sensitive to current developments, and even sometimes accelerate them, by seeking a theological covering note for social change. The crisis in the clergy complements the crisis in the parish. As the example from the Brazilian shanty town indicates, parish institutions which once supported each other under the single priestly eye tend to become institutions with single objectives more easily led by laymen. Not only that, but the state tends to take over some of these roles[1] or else they are carried out by voluntary associations having little or nothing to do with the Church. The mutually supporting functions of the parish disintegrate and the priest's role undergoes a corresponding disintegration. The priest may indeed take up a political role, or assist a scheme of land settlement, or go into education and the media, but it occurs to him that he may as well perform these social tasks as a layman equipped with the appropriate expertise. Welfare is a Christian duty but it does not need a sacerdotal vocation. Moreover the motivations to social work are as capable of being expressed in humanistic as in Christian terms.

At the higher social levels the priest encounters a further erosion of his superior educational position. There may, of course, be a long tradition of anti-intellectualism on the part of the Church, as in Spain, or a history of social conflict over education as in France and (to a lesser degree) Belgium. At any rate the priest no longer plays the role of major interpreter of the world. On the other hand there are countries where sections of the educated laity desire to work in concert with the Church. Theology, in Greece or in England, is largely a lay activity. An organization like Zoë in Greece or Znak in Poland complements the efforts of the clerical caste. Openings to the world and to the left can be explored by Christian intellectuals. In Spain the impulse to modernity is carried through the lay order of Opus Dei, and within a conservative format even performs functions equivalent to those performed elsewhere by the Protestant Ethic.

The changes currently affecting the clergy are very much part of the process of social differentiation which is perhaps the area where the theory of secularization can be expressed most coherently. In other words, the notion of secularization has a relatively clear purchase on social reality when it indicates the separation of different spheres of life from ecclesiastical control, whether it be scientific endeavour, or social welfare or ideological legitimation. It is interesting that in the last mentioned sphere even the final bastions of Church-State unity are under pressure. In Spain, for example, where the 800 years' war forged an intense union of Church and state, the Church has at last emerged as a channel of criticism. In Brazil sections of the hierarchy are highly critical of the present régime. At the international level, of course, the churches have moved very far from the role of ideological legitimation and are persistent critics of the faults of liberal democracy, to a degree which must cause some confusion in the suburban constituencies whence they draw their principal grass-roots support. In Eastern Europe it remains true that while the churches are both subject to repression and/or to subsidized control they constitute the only area of autonomy and almost the only channel of political dissent with regard to the monolithic, totalitarian state. In Eastern Europe they are the refuge of the marginal, the excluded, the relatively unhonoured, the independent and the carriers of long-term cultural continuities. They are, of course, mostly separated from the state, and the privatization which often occurs in the west is officially required of them.

The impact of differentiation is dramatically illustrated in Quebec, particularly as it affects the social comment of the Church. Quebec is instructive because it is another of those areas, like Poland, Ireland and the Basque country, where Catholicism has had to stand in for the state as the guardian of ethnic, linguistic and cultural identity. Quebec is France without the revolution and therefore of special interest. It is, as M. Lemieux has argued, a case of a modern, urbanizing society possessed by the values of consumption and affluence, which yet sustains a traditional leadership. Once again we have an instance of a Church which is institutionally strong but which faces normative divergence.

Up to 1949 Church and State had mutually imprinted stigmata on each other; their positions in the social structure had been isomorphic from head to foot. Then social conflicts occurred which were not susceptible to being cast in the framework of religiously coloured nationalism. Furthermore, in its relations with government the Church was confronted not by explicit anti-clericalism or direct rejection of its values, but by criteria of bureaucratic efficiency asserted in this or that defined area of specific competence such as the sphere of education. A technicist mentality at the professional level was complemented by social disorganization at the level of the ordinary parish. The Church was under pressure as the mediator of local solidarities transmitted upward through hierarchical structures. As a result its language, theology and liturgical forms underwent a transmutation. Forms which had expressed an exterior order and necessity comparable to the natural order now expressed a direct approach of 'I' to 'You' based on mutual participation. The clergy sought out each other and the people in primary groups. The idea of the Creator-God (who might well be identified with a creation dominated by the practice of American Protestantism) shifted towards the idea of a loving, participating God whose natural social expression was in popular solidarity, even perhaps in the practice of syndicalism.

The quiet internal revolution did not necessarily achieve a political correlative. But it is interesting that the Church, like sections of the university population, has now become an area where changes in culture are symbolized and signalled at a quite early stage. The Church, living increasingly in the sphere of values and symbols rather than the structures of power, is no longer the last part of society to move. Its clergy even shift with the seismic sensitivity of the marginal intellectual. It is in this context that Mueller's comments on the way ritual change can be detected before social change have a special interest. Certainly in England the Church was affected before the Universities. However, the problem of a language with which to speak to the wider society rapidly arises. Once the blanket terminology of legitimation is abandoned one is left either with very high order values of no immediate and obvious application or else the highly unrealistic situational vocabulary of the militant cell. Naturally, it is perfectly possible and increasingly normal to talk the language of group interest in the manner of one association amongst others. The difficulty is to locate a critical vocabulary for on-going political issues of the middle range without being hopelessly compromised in everyday political activity. Eternal verity and political contingency sort ill together.

For some there is no such difficulty. Not merely in Quebec, but in Holland, France, Italy, Spain, indeed almost everywhere, there have appeared communities of militants, often including militant clergy, who combine a situational personalism with a politicized theology. They sit loose to the Church but can use its highly general symbolism for an equally general critique of exploitation and repression, whether in the third world or in the first world. The former sometimes leads them to the latter. Politics can be consumed in prophecy, in which case the difficulties and compromises of political contingency no longer matter. Personal values and human equality can be freely affirmed and the appropriate structures created without the problem of running a large-scale technical society being faced in responsible practice. Groups of Christian militants can act politically and at the same time convert the highly personal and communal symbols of Christianity into lived present realities, including the euphoric expectation of the open eschatological future. The deposit of Christian individualism remains above all in the supposition that the New Society will need New Men if it is not to be corrupted from the start. Perhaps it is also present in the tendency, noted by Nesti, to see change as dependent on the discovery of a personal, intimate, ludic sacred sphere, in spite of the rejection of any notion of a separate devotional sector. Perhaps the Dutch group 'Shalom' most dramatically illustrates the process whereby unity in Christ and ecumenical aspiration is translated into pan-human universalism. It also represents an interesting attempt at creating a dynamic changing live centre without compromising the core of its mission or smudging its boundaries with 'the world'. The Italian movement 'Dissenso' has something of the same character, as have many of the French movements. The same phenomenon clearly occurs on the margin of French Jewry. Occasionally the radical impulse has expressed itself in terms of adherence to left wing political parties, usually those of the new extreme left. Holland and France both furnish examples. But in general party politics are seen as belonging to the old order, both in West and East.

It is a natural transition from the communitarian and personalist enthusiasms of the militants to the pietist revivals, whether these take the form of the Jesus movement, the new Pietism reported by Sihvo in Finland, or the Pentecostalist movement without and within the churches. Such developments constitute a 'bridge passage' in that they mediate between the old and the new, filling the new forms with old wine. Quite clearly there is a continuity of atmosphere though not of personnel and institutions between modern charismatics and older-style revivalism. In any case, the old-style revivalists rarely set much store by institutional continuities and boundaries. The spirit enabled them to recognize the works of the spirit wherever they might occur. The bridge passage between old and new is also evident in the restoration of social disciplines and the repeated reports of rehabilitation after a period spent in the drug culture. Indeed, in the Unified Family, which lies apart from the charismatics in its syncretic tendency, much more than social discipline is restored, since it is quite clear that restitutionist elements are present and an appeal to traditional national mythology. This traditionalism is present, at least in the sphere of morals, amongst British charismatics. Amongst them the general ecological concern about environmental pollution is translated back into a concern with moral pollution. The British Festival of Light is led by traditionalists concerned with the erosion of moral standards and followed by enthusiastic charismatics.

It is interesting that the traditional guardians of the Protestant Ethic, notably the Methodist Church itself, are too liberalized and rationalized to share in the charismatic renewal to any extent. Like most liberal denominations in the U.K. and the U.S.A. they share in a relative decline. Maybe small injections of the spirit in childhood prevent any large-scale epidemic in early adulthood. But they are not entirely immune. One cannot ignore success, and whereas the previous wave of converts to the Witnesses and the Mormons clearly had no resonance for the older denominations the present wave of Pentecostalism has. A church so well organized on bureaucratic principles as Methodism may well join in the general flight from bureaucracy. Hence the current move to scrap the use of agendas. As in the Church of England so in Methodism the new recruits to the depleted ministry are disproportionately drawn from the ranks of those influenced by the charismatic movement. Furthermore, whereas the ecumenical movement is both unpopular and bureaucratic in its institutional expression the grass roots ecumenism of the spirit has a greater appeal.

Séguy explicitly interprets the wave of Pentecostalism within the historical context of Pietism and Methodism, and within the context of interpretation suggested by Halévy. Almost he persuades me. Pentecostalists are to the radical communities as Methodism was to the Anabaptist movement. Methodism and Pentecostalism represent a compromise. Beyond that one would want to ask whether the new religions in Japan do not represent a similar compromise. They seem highly susceptible to an interpretation of the Halévy type.[2] Certainly in Chile one can see that Pentecostalism represents a socially stabilizing influence, though its apolitical stance may weaken its impact on political life. The shift that Sihvo notes in successive Finnish revivals from symbolic protest to a kind of traditionalism fits Séguy's analysis. Indeed, it is interesting to note that small Christian parties have occurred in the Scandinavian countries, drawing their support largely from the old Pietist movements but also to some extent from the modern ones. There may be a difference in that the older ones were largely agrarian while the latest waves of Pietism are urban. The Christian parties represent an evangelical piety which has left the centre of society where it was once dominant (as in the reign of Christian VI or for that matter the court of Queen Victoria) to migrate to the peripheries. The great population centres have been left to the bureaucratic administration, to the liberal media and to the counter-culture, including the charismatics and the Jesus People. This is exactly the picture provided by Nuy's paper on Amsterdam.

Pentecostalism and the Jesus People movement share other features in common in varying degrees. The attitude to institutions is similar: institutions kill but the spirit giveth life. The attitude to rationalism is also similar: the Bible is interpreted in strictly fundamentalist fashion. The Jesus People leave the body of society *and* the chaos of the counter-culture by reintegrating themselves into communes. The Pentecostalists leave the body of society in another sense, by achieving direct communication beyond the barriers of language. Just as the counter-culture feels any elegant, structured speech to be an offence against spontaneity so religious spontaneity attempts to transcend the restrictions of language. Like some of the effects of drugs which reduce the person to a pre-social level of oceanic identity the gift of tongues may be neuro-physiologically regressive but it symbolizes the same hope of transcending cultures and social roles. As for the conditions facilitating such phenomena these may of course vary considerably. Séguy relates Neo-Pentecostalism within the Roman Church to a lay-clerical conflict over leadership and to the disorientation following the Vatican Council. Where bureaucratic authority falters charismatic authority may take its place. Richardson's account of the Jesus People leans on the notion of a blockage at the political practical level which canalizes frustration into religious forms. It is the downward curve where Shalom represents the upward curve. Certainly the Jesus People seem to have picked up much of the flotsam of the Student Movement rather as Quakerism acted as the residual religious legatee of the English Revolution.

Both Pentecostalism and the Jesus People function to provide something of a substitute family for those uprooted from families of origin.

The Unified Family (or 'The Holy Spirit Association for the

Unification of World Christianity') clearly has links with the themes mentioned: the social functions of the substitute family, links with traditional views and spiritual aspiration.[3] But it includes a syncretistic aspect which connects it to movements like Bahai. Indeed both its founder and the Persian originator of Bahai pursued lives with clear similarities to the Messiahship of Christ in the context of Far Eastern religions and of Islam. Beckford notes the authoritarianism of this group which is parallel to that noted earlier amongst Scientologists and also to the Commune of the Word as described by Nuy. This word is not one of the dead words of a language but the living word of an adolescent Indian guru. He gives a word realized by interior meditation beyond the seductions of reason and science.

Syncretism can easily be part of the general pan-human aspirations found in such groups as Shalom and in the student movement generally. In the Unified Family it takes the form of claiming to link oriental philosophy and Christianity, East and West. The same tendency is found in the mystical transcendence of all culturally specific roles. The pregnant silences of Zen are a rebuke to all the specificities of language as well as to ratiocination. The oriental influence takes many forms: Hare Krishna, Transcendental Meditation, different varieties of Yoga, and it runs parallel to similar tendencies in England during the outbreak of social radicalism in the 1930s. No doubt the oriental tendency is reinforced by a political preference for the third world. But the current of mystical divorce from the institutional Church is not in itself at all new, nor is the connection with radicalism. For example, the radical premonitions of the Reformation were much influenced by the Theologia Germanica. When one considers the characteristics of that variety of mysticism its contemporary analogues are clear. The reserve towards the Incarnation and the body of the Church, the identification of the Beatific Vision with one's own experience, the ethical indifferentism, the deliverance from imperfection by illumination, are all closely paralleled in much of the contemporary addiction to ecstasy.

Mysticism in its pure form is a kind of invisible religion. But 'invisible religion' as we have come to understand it has varied meanings. It may be the 'self-steered systems of relevance' which Luckmann believes characteristic of modern man. Or it may be the inchoate, inarticulate cultural pieties described by Salomonsen and elsewhere researched by Towler in his work on 'Common Religion'. It is often forgotten just how recently parts of Europe were evangelized, how political and dynastic the reasons for evangelization sometimes were, and how long and sometimes superficial was the process of religious change. Underneath has lain what I have called a 'subterranean theology' which still provides much of the workaday understanding of everyday exigencies. Vast sections of the population are still part of a common Afro-European religion and are pre-Christian rather than post-Christian in their beliefs. Their notions are dominated both by cosmic fairness and cosmic fate and by techniques for averting physical and psychic danger. Even their understanding of the major Christian rites is soaked in these notions, and the efficacy of Christian faith is judged by the pragmatic criteria of the old religion. This situation resembles that currently obtaining in Africa both in its syncretism and in the persistent pragmatic secularity which informs the judgement of what kind of religion is worth having. One hears the authentic voice of this inarticulate stratum of belief in the response to a question asked by Towler. 'I have them all christened. (prompt: Why?). Don't know. People have it done. It keeps them safe like wearing a St. Christopher.' Things are done and children are 'done', as Salomonsen has argued, because they have been done and give protection. The same is true of the widespread recourse to prayer: people observing the changes and chances of the world and the vulnerability of their children appeal to the protecting powers. They claim prayer as a protection just as they claim the label 'Christian' as an outward sign of basic ethical decency. That this underground stream of primitive pragmatism, half hope and half fatalistic despair, has persisted for a long time is very clear from the recent researches of Keith Thomas on the beliefs of sixteenth- and seventeenth-century England. Defections from the institutional Church and adherence to the incoherent hopes of proverbial culture, not to mention quasi-scientific determinisms like astrology and palmistry are not in any way new. This layer of 'common religion' is strikingly homogeneous and underlies the apparent plurality of all faiths and none even in large mobile expanding centres such as Amsterdam and Copenhagen. Indeed, one may even argue that the vigorous denominationalism of Victorian England or nineteenth-century America offered a more vital pluralism than the cultural inertias currently exerting their power. How pluralistic *is* a religious situation which contains virulent nationalisms, the common religion just mentioned, the homogenizing socialization of socialist societies?

Civic Religion is quite different to 'invisible religion' in that it is highly visible and indeed is defined by visibility. It provides the overarching symbols and rituals of our civic, indeed of our civilized, existence. Naturally, it is very much corroded by the penchant for personal expression and spontaneity and compromised by its association with powers that be. Nevertheless, it comes to life in the great civic and national occasions and exercises an appeal to enormous numbers of people who know nothing of the complex web of meanings hidden behind the luminosity of the ritual action and the elegant beauty of the language. It provides the highest form of public rhetoric and as such succumbs to the feeling against all formality and against all ritual clothes, especially when worn by emperors. The desire for ritual nakedness is against it, but its decline generates some of the longing for rituals which will reclothe the bare utility informing many personal relationships.

I conclude with a group of themes largely drawn from Weber, some of which are mediated through the paper by Peel. Peel's reflections are paradoxical, and rooted in the paradox of Africa itself: rural communities whose religiosity may resemble early medieval Europe, and national states which are often as 'secular' as contemporary America. Firstly, he argues that world religions, Christianity included, are defined less by their morality than by their myths and symbols and the models they provide of man, God and society. Current moral divergence from official norms may not therefore be particularly significant. At any rate the contemporary divergence is different from but not greater than the contrast between official Catholicism and the practice of feudal society. In short, religions adapt yet do not necessarily lose their character. Secondly, he points to the way Christianity wars against itself and is its own grave digger. It is its own grave digger with respect to the 'disenchantment' of the world of which it is one major carrier amongst others. And it wars against itself through symbols and perspectives which subvert any institutional realization it may achieve. The vision must be incorporated in a human body and a social body, but it is wider than any social institution can bear. So sectarian and utopian groups constantly translate the potent remainders of Christian theology. This process whereby ecclesiastical notions are both earthed and made impossibly visionary is endemic. The tension provides the dynamism of Christian civilizations over against the long-term continuities of common religion and civic cults.

The underlying theme has been Weberian: the growth of bureaucracy, long-term planning, sectionalization, impersonality, technical rationality, disenchantment. The defining characteristics of the religious development we have described have largely been opposed to the bureaucratic tendency. They have attempted to recover personality, wholeness, the affective sources of illumination and enchantment. The peculiar difficulty of institutional Christianity and its opportunity has been the dialectic of its relation to the Weberian tendency: the fact that it is partly a carrier of rationality, bureaucracy and disenchantment and yet denies that these things are all that can be known or that they exhaust the possibilities of transcendence and mystery.

Notes

1. Poland, for complex reasons, is a partial exception. There the shift from country to town occurs within a complex of institutions largely provided by the Church.
2. They are, of course, much more this-worldly, instrumental and political than Pentecostalism.
3. For an extensive analysis of the Unified Family (or Unification Church) see Eileen Barker: 'Living the Divine Principle', *Archives des Sciences Sociales des Religions*, September 1978.

IV

Mutations: Religio-Political Crisis and the Collapse of Puritanism and Humanism

In this essay I am concerned with the nature of the student movement and I wish to deal in particular with the political attitudes of that movement by referring to the religious aspect of the discussion. If we want to understand why it is that student attitudes are only marginally political then one must look at them as a form of religiosity. The modern Brethren of the Free Spirit, virtuosi of ecstasy and experiental freedom, necessarily reject the contingent, pragmatic, constricting, disciplined character of political action.

To set out the religious aspect involves attention to the theme of secularization and to what has happened to two key elements in the ideological underpinning of the university: humanism (both as a life-style and as a rationalistic approach to religion) and the Protestant Ethic. I will be concerned with how humanism came to be stigmatized as irrelevant and élitist and how the Protestant Ethic came to be linked with the evils of industrial society, and the misuse of science.

There are two points which I want to make at the outset in order to make clearer the intellectual strategy I am employing. The first is that I cannot hope to deal with the whole of what is called the student movement, since it extended over a very wide variety of societies with very different systems of higher education and different types of social problems. I shall be concerned with very broad developments as I have experienced them in an Anglo-American setting. This means that I am describing and criticizing trends in affluent, democratic Protestant societies. Clearly, to the extent that student movements operate in societies which are neither affluent nor Protestant nor democratic, my analysis would have to be modified very considerably. In Italy, for example, an interest in magic would be seen as a phenomenon of the extreme right not the extreme left.

HISTORICAL BACKGROUND

The principal difference, so far as historical background is concerned, between Protestant and Catholic societies is the degree to which intellectuals in the latter have been anti-clerical and opposed to the political power of a monolithic ecclesiastical institution. In Protestant societies there is no historical background of an anti-clerical or indeed of a Marxist intelligentsia. So far as Britain is concerned there was some intellectual commitment to a rationalism in the mid-nineteenth century, an interest in socialist ideas from the 1880s onwards and an element of Marxism during the crisis of the 1930s. But on the whole, the dominant style even amongst left-wing intellectuals has been one concerned with the gradual elimination of social evils and the extension of personal liberties. The dominant theme has been the peace issue and on this issue collaboration between non-religious and believing intellectuals has been particularly easy. Both have respected what they believed to be the benign figure of a liberal-socialist Jesus and have assumed that the New Testament is a pacifist manifesto about building 'Jerusalem in England's green and pleasant land'. And one has to remember that the religion which they espoused was not usually conceived by them in terms of a strong institution, but rather as a set of images, visions and ideals. If they rejected the institution of the Church it was often more a rejection of the public school chapel than the Church of

England itself. Even institutional religion presented no special dividing line among intellectuals: after all non-conformist churches had always tended to espouse the peace issue and the Catholic party in the Church of England notoriously possessed a vigorous socialist wing. In any case the Church of England as a whole was not so strong as to make the issue of institutional religion a major focus of attention. So the position of intellectuals *vis-à-vis* religion is easily summarized: adhesion or lack of it to the institutional church was not a major dividing line and along the poorly defined margins of belief, half-belief and non-belief there was a general reverence for a liberal-socialist Jesus and the progressive tenets embodied in the gospels. All instructed intellectuals knew that Jesus was against war and riches, and if for some of them he happened to be God as well that only showed how right they were to agree with him.

Now, I think it is probably true to say that this complex of attitudes lasted up until the end of the 1950's. The last major expression of such attitudes was the movement to ban the atom bomb: the Campaign for Nuclear Disarmament. In this campaign the usual elements of the 'responsible', liberal-minded middle class were well to the fore and made their usual point: Britain must set a moral example to the world. In other words the progressive and educated section of the middle class once more showed a characteristic concern for a moral issue focussed on foreign policy. To that extent their attitudes were a final expression of Britain's imperial past, when British policy might have had an important influence on the world. But bringing up the rear behind the representatives of the middle-class conscience was the shape of things to come. The 'ban the bomb' marches were a kind of gypsy caravanserai in which the mobile, relaxed style of a new youth culture was clearly evident. The newspapers took especial care to focus on the bizarre tail of long-haired troubadours who made up a substantial part of the marchers. Amongst these troubadours the overlap between student culture and the culture of pop music was particularly clear. Now, it is not my object to go into this increasing symbiosis between the student way of life and 'pop music': it has been adequately analysed elsewhere. Suffice to say that after the failure of the ban-the-bomb movement the troubadours gradually took over from the 'responsible' educated middle class and began to adopt an expressionistic, vitalist, semi-mystical style. This style became more and more opposed to education, more especially the values of science and rationality. It posed the subjective person against the objectivist world of science and against the objective organization of society, identifying science as part of the social and political establishment.

Now, this is the point at which I must introduce my second point designed to clarify the intellectual strategy behind my remarks. This revulsion against science can be seen as a crucial element in the development of the intelligentsia *vis-à-vis* religion and the 'secularization process', so-called. Up to the 1950s the liberal, progressive middle class had contained certain secular elements, even though religion was not a crucial issue. After all, it adopted a rationalistic approach to social problems: it desired better social engineering. It contributed to better knowledge about society: the London School of Economics was one of its achievements. It might be further argued (though it is a matter of definition and debate) that to concentrate on the ethical aspects of the New Testament and to make religion a set of cultural ideals rather than institutional and dogmatic loyalty was a move towards secularity. Certainly, this section of the middle class tended to be moralistic rather than ritualistic and to combine a rationalist liberalism with a secularized Puritanism. On these criteria one might say that important elements in the progressive middle class were semi-secularized.

But I have already mentioned the socialist emphasis in the Anglo-Catholic wing of the Church of England. In the figure of someone like William Morris this overlapped an anarchistic, utopian strain of socialism, concerned to recover the right relation of the arts to society. It tapped the alienation of the artistic intelligentsia from a capitalistic society whose main criterion of worth appeared to be utility. It linked with the feeling of those who felt engulfed by vast centralizing bureaucracies and who were anxious to maintain local customs, and to regain the élan of life in small communities. For these people science was often regarded as an ally of the Puritan ethic and a major component in an ugly industrial civilization indifferent to life and beauty. For people who saw the Puritan ethic in this light Catholic civilization seemed more integral, more rooted in genuine community, more conducive to art and beauty. Thus science, Puritanism, industrial society and utilitarian ugliness became linked together as mutually supporting evils. For some middle-class people their rejection of these evils took the form of conversion to Catholicism, for others it spawned a philosophy of art for the sake of art. The sensations of beauty supplanted the imperatives of morality. Both Catholicism and aestheticism were influential in the 1890s and they were augmented by a margin of eastern mysticism.

It was *this* strain of progressive feeling which lay behind the appearance of a new youth culture in the wake of the ban-the-bomb marches. This culture was anarchic, morally deviant and experimental, aesthetically exploratory, mystical. In the 1890s, of course, this deviant style was confined to a relatively small section of society. But in the situation which arose after the Second World War it became available to a much wider social segment. Higher education expanded very rapidly. Initially the mood was rather quietist, even conformist. Certainly even political liberals were not particularly nonconformist in their cultural style. Those who were on the far left in the sense of adhering to the authoritarian Marxism of that period were often culturally Puritan.

THE COLLAPSE OF PURITANISM

But then three developments occurred. First, the appeal of neo-Puritan, authoritarian, atheistic Marxism collapsed, more particularly after the invasion of Hungary and the revelations about the appalling brutalities perpetrated by the Communist régime in Russia. Adulation of Russia by the Communist left largely ceased. The problem became one of devising a socialism which had a genuinely human face, and when Czechoslovakia followed Hungary it seemed impossible that any human face could appear behind the iron curtain. Thus the Puritan ethic at home and the Puritan ethos of authoritarian socialism abroad fell into equal disrepute. Any discipline of the self, as in classical Puritanism, any discipline in society as exemplified in Marxist régimes was rejected. All authority was labelled 'authoritarian', all centralized decision or decision by older people and by experts was automatically ruled out as paternalistic.[1]

With this double collapse of Puritan values went the other two developments I mentioned: the appearance of a pop-culture appealing to the young in general through the mass media and the growth of a vastly expanded university population educated as if they were to be part of an élite or part of a leisured class. Pop-culture I leave on one side, except to refer to the obvious: the link with the deprived culture of the American negro, and the 'protest' element which achieved its first predominance in the public eye through Bob Dylan. My main concern here is with the young people who made up the expanded university population in a situation where the imperatives of the cold war had been weakened, where money was available and where military service had been abolished.

These young people had literally nothing to fear and had been brought up in atmospheres where whatever they did they were not subject to serious consequences for their actions. From school and home to university their environment was easy and supportive in a way no environment had ever been in the history of mankind, apart that is from the very rich. Many of them had been brought up in systems of progressive education which assumed that life consisted of personal exploration not of tasks and challenges. I can develop this later, but at this juncture it is relevant to one single point: large numbers of people were given an education based on the style developed in élite schools by the semi-anarchic section of the middle class. Such middle-class people were often concentrated in key positions in the education system and encouraged their own free style within the state schools. Now this meant that by the time young people reached university, and encountered its extremely open and traditionally liberal atmosphere, they had been trained to anticipate levels of self-fulfilment which even the university could not provide and to which society in general was largely indifferent. They had been given humanist tastes without the availability of humanist roles. They had been taught to relax and found a world still at work and schools where there were still tests of competence. In short, they became candidates for educated unemployment. Only one further element needs to be added: the politics of conventional reform through the central structures of society moved but slowly and were plainly controlled by the reality-principle. For young people brought up on the pleasure-principle an alternative had to be found to conventional politics and this was provided by the student movement, in particular by its concern with psychic subversion of everything to do with the Puritan cultural style. Curiously enough, this tactic worked on the principle of social salvation adopted by Puritan evangelists: each one convert one, or, if you like, each one contaminate one. Psychic subversion took the place of political reform, iconography took over from carefully argued political programmes. What static icons were to religion, casual graffiti and explosions of paint were to student ideology.

The point to begin with is the erosion of the character-structure of Puritanism. My main thesis will be concerned with the way a classical Protestantism, based on discipline and 'works', indeed on disciplined work, has been attacked by the anarchism which goes back first of all to the Romantic movement and Rousseau but ultimately to the anarchic, radical wing of the Protestant Reformation. Weber's Protestant Ethic has been suborned by an antinomian theology based on faith alone. Yet this doctrine of faith *alone* is different from the

Reformation doctrine, since the radical implications of faith alone were normally controlled by the fact that the extremists among the reformers were concerned with faith *in Christ* alone and they usually added sola scriptura to sola fide. The modern extension of the Reformation has become just a celebration of faith for which there is no *object* of faith. It is a *pure* subjectivism. With this general and over-simplified thesis stated let us look at the ways in which the 'Puritan Ethic' has been eroded. We have a situation where the subjectivism of the extreme, antinomian wing of the Reformation is conjoined with elements derived from Catholic culture and above all with anarchic mysticism, much of it now more easily based on eastern sources than anything contaminated by the cultural history of Europe.

What do we mean by the Protestant Ethic? Many things, but in this context I mean guilt and work, and above all guilt about not working. Protestant character structure was based on literacy, self-improvement, conscience, saving, thrift, paying one's way, preparing for the future, personal control, honest dealing, veracity. It was pragmatic and empirical, dedicated to practicality, utility and hard fact. It appealed to common sense: and in doing so it overlapped an important strain in Anglo-American philosophy. This syndrome of virtues became otiose with welfare and affluence at least for part of the educated young and a section of the youth culture. At the university they encountered a life-style which contained certain of these Protestant virtues, but which included more aristocratic values of relaxation, aesthetic appreciation, contemplation. Disproportionate numbers of those socialized in old Puritan styles entered the university because their self-discipline enabled them to succeed in the education system. And alongside them came those who had been reared in the new 'progressive' style of education and large numbers affected by the relaxed values of the general youth culture. Unfortunately, most of those who entered into the humanistic inheritance of the university were unable to stay there. You cannot have an élite of hundreds of thousands. The scientists were employable, the humanists were not, or else they were forced to practise what some of them thought a low-grade form of humanism through school-teaching. Thus they felt cheated and the semi-monastic disciplines of a contemplative style were stigmatized as irrelevant. They had been encouraged to pass judgement on the universe but their destiny was a limited and limiting role. Industry seemed unrewarding and industrial vocations appeared sordid. Being failed aristocrats and thwarted humanists they despised commerce. So they turned either to personal exploration outside the disciplines of the university or else rejected contemplation in favour of a union of theory and political practice. They would educate themselves by the practice of subversion and in that respect humanism provided very little guidance. It was, as they said, irrelevant. Parenthetically, one must note that their own personalist philosophy also proved irrelevant. Whenever they tried to organize they were confronted by the necessity of authority and discipline. This proved impossible to achieve, and even the most authoritarian student organizations which attempted a secular version of the Puritan character, foundered on the question of authority. Would-be Leninism found no characterological base on which to operate.

What has been said makes it quite clear why conventional politics have very little appeal. Messianism has no commerce with political pragmatism, and messianic aspirations for total liberty are affronted by the limitations on personal freedom inherent in the political role. The politician must take what shifting balance of advantages are available, jettison his personal life and even some of his beliefs for the wider cause.

The exigencies of party organization or of any coherent political grouping demand discipline. Moreover, this discipline is exercised in the context of the two largest and most impersonal forms of modern organization: the bureaucracy and the state. Size and impersonality are the two most anathematized features of contemporary liberal society and hence the almost total withdrawal of student revivalists from the political scene.

Furthermore, of course, they believe not only that conventional politics are ineffective but also positively responsible for the evils of the world, above all Vietnam. Political action in Parliaments is the arena of corruption and pure souls and pure persons should have no part in it.

THE COLLAPSE OF HUMANISM

I now turn more precisely to the relationship between student culture and humanism, particularly so far as the question of religion is concerned. I use the word humanism in two senses. The first sense is easily dealt with: humanism defined as a devotion to the human as distinct from the divine. This kind of humanism is continuous with the rationalist and ethical societies of the nineteenth century and is concerned to show that orthodox religion is incompatible with reason and science and detracts from human autonomy. Humanists of this kind hold that ethical standards are properly achieved not by virtue of transcendental rewards or divine edicts but by responsible choice of what is recognized as inherently good or of what is appropriate to the best and richest kind of human life. Of course, the humanist movement, though always against orthodox Christianity, has wavered between attempting to find a ritual and emotional substitute for religion and rejecting everything to do with religious forms. It was always ready to join with the reformist, progressive wing of Christianity in ethical crusades, and often the moral outlook of reformist Christians and Puritanical atheists and agnostics was very similar. Both the Christian progressives and Puritan agnostics tended to recruit from the middle class. A movement like Unitarianism, which flourished in the nineteenth century and now languishes, combined the two. There is, however, only one thing to be said about this type of humanism: its moral outlook has been by-passed and its devotion to science and reason deprives it of interest. Humanist societies used to have quite an appeal to students, but they now have about as much éclat as a liberal minded body like the Student Christian Movement. The S.C.M. fell a victim to its own 'openness'. It espoused the early stages of the present style and thereby destroyed itself, leaving the field to the closed cells of the Christian Union. Liberalism taken beyond a certain point plays into the hands of right and left extremes.

The second sense of humanism refers to the life-style of the academic and the intellectual in so far as it relates to the ideal of Renaissance Man. More narrowly this kind of humanism connotes a culture rooted in the classics. This ideal and this culture found no great difficulty in co-existing with a rather aristocratic, stoical variant of Christianity. After all, Christian civilization had harboured the classics in its monasteries and Latin was its language. True, the Renaissance had included an explicit theoretical extension of secular political realism and an unbridled celebration of the individual, but it had also combined Christianity and the life-enhancing arts together in some of the sublimest achievements of civilized man. So there was no great difficulty in combining a stoic, civilized and civic ethos with a proper regard for Christian decencies.

Humanism in this mode is now as much under pressure as the kind of humanism which is devoted to science and reason. It is clear that any acquaintance with the classical civilization is rapidly disappearing and the use of a combination of Roman stoicism and Christian ethics to socialize the young is now barely possible, even in public schools. But the erosion of humanism goes much further than this: not only is the tradition of the classics forgotten but the very notions of a 'classic' and of a tradition are in disrepute. History itself is devalued and replaced by sociology. The urge towards relevance rejects cultural standards and continuities. Moreover, humanism involved the notion of a discipline, particularly grammar and rhetoric, and while today grammar is condemned for formalism, rhetoric is condemned as hypocritical. This occurs because an ideology of the naked person celebrates immediacy and therefore has to reject standards which are imparted from the past and cannot see the point of mastering rules which have no personal appeal. Such an ideology holds that ordered, elegant speech is treason against the existential vagaries of genuine emotion. This means, incidentally, that so far as religion is concerned there is a prejudice against the ordered formality of divine worship. A collapse in humanist cultural standards can mean a rebellion against traditional beauty in the ordering of liturgy. Where classics are despised, access to a whole tradition of speech is made more difficult. Indeed, speech itself becomes suspect. Humanism is the attitude of the scribe and the scribes are rejected on the ground that they are Pharisees. In a way this runs parallel to the rejection of Puritanism. Puritans delighted in the Word, humanists delighted in words; Puritans studied scripture, humanists studied manuscripts. But the new anarchistic personalism despised both sermons and speeches and aspired to a condition of all-round reaction in which words and music, sight, sound and touch are one.

When the devotee of the youth cult rejects the rational and cumulative ordering of words he rejects a sequential mode of thought and the notion of logical argument. Words also involve categories and categories divide up the world of experience when in his view the world should be experienced as a whole. It is this desire to embrace the world as a *totality* which spills over into naturalistic mysticism. The devotee of personalism falls into a relationship with the 'All' and because this defies rational expression he can only witness to the overwhelming nature of the experience without being able to give an account of it. Like the oriental mystic he can only ejaculate the word 'Om'. Like the Zen adept his religion defies both categories and expression. The ineffable can only be expressed in inconsequential nonsense. The pregnant silence of Zen complements the augmented decibels of pop music production, designed to 'stone people out of their minds'. Since the religious adept experiences the world as a totality and as a totality preceding words and categories he is effectively returned to the world of the new-born infant: a world of uninterrupted noise or uninterrupted silence. As we shall see later this return to angel-infancy is an important motif in contemporary student religion. Infancy is amoral and natural, and nudity is an appropriate symbol for an ideology of infantile delinquency. This condition is exactly the reverse of the mature, ordered, rational and acquired autonomy desired by humanists.

There is, however, one particular in which the youth culture seems to resemble classical humanism, and that is its desire to relate the knowledge gained in particular disciplines within a universal perspective. It desires a total view of the world. This is why student ideologies ransack one discipline after another to produce a general perspective showing how everything is related to everything else. The phenomenon of left-wing functionalism is interesting here. Functionalists like Parsons showed the systemic and (perhaps) beneficent interrelation of social structures. Radicals accepted this over-integrated view of society, differing only in their estimate of its beneficence. The ecumenical movement of the intellect can look like a proper disdain for artificial boundaries, but it is actually part of the fear of categories. Levels of judgement are confused; the specific grain of different subjects is ignored; fact and desire are jumbled together; no considerations are possible based on more or less, or a calculation of if *this* then not *that*. All that is necessary is a chanting of the favourite slogans of the youth cult. And one of the most important of these slogans is the notion that all knowledge is absolutely relative. Total relevance ends up in total relativity. There is no external knowledge or reality 'out there' which can impose itself on the sacred psyche. Just as there is no God 'out there' so there is no external world. Everything should be malleable to the demands of personal vision. If it is not malleable one can retire into a world where the visionary becomes real: the world of drugs. Thus the attempt to encompass all knowledge ends up in a denial of the possibility of knowledge, just as the attempt to achieve total communication concludes in a scepticism about the possibility of making contact. The susceptibility to drugs links, of course, to the espousal of naturalistic mysticism. Similarly, the scepticism about rational knowledge concerning the world plays back into fideism. It is only a short step from extreme scepticism to salvation by faith alone. When reason fails what is left but faith?

POWERS OF LIGHT AND POWERS OF DARKNESS

So far I have discussed tendencies which are favourable to religion in general but not particularly to Christianity. After all Christianity is a historical religion and the ahistorical nature of the youth consciousness is hostile to it. Moreover, Christianity, at least in some forms, is in favour of reason, and though it has had its moments of conflict with science it has recognized the importance of objective knowledge about the universe. Indeed, it is one of the complaints of contemporary radicals that Christianity has too easily embraced the ideal of scientific truth. Christianity further involves a moral outlook, a continuing commitment to a defined and bounded religious community and an attempt to give an intellectual account of itself, all of which are contrary to an ideology of the unrestrained self. So in all these respects Christianity is under pressure. In other respects, however, it finds points of congruence with the new cultural mode.

The most obvious case is the Jesus People and overlapping movements like the Festival of Light. In the Festival of Light the salvationism of the young is linked to an attempt by more staid, older people to control the spread of pornography. By a concession to the contemporary style pornography is labelled 'moral pollution'. The appeal to youth is primarily through a lively, charismatic mode of evangelism remote from conventional Christianity though not, of course, from the tradition of American evangelism. 'Jesus' becomes a 'happening' and above all so in the immensely popular musicals *Godspell* and *Jesus Christ Superstar*. The Jesus Christ of these productions is a contemporary 'Lord of the Dance'. Nevertheless it is worth remarking that the Jesus People form a link back to traditional American culture, though their anti-intellectualism probably disqualifies them from full contact with the university tradition.

One of the major events of the hippie culture life-style is the pilgrimage to Glastonbury Tor, traditionally the most sacred spot in England to which Joseph of Arimathea is believed to have brought the Christ child. The Glastonbury cult lies closer to the Christian pattern in several ways. It invokes a saviour figure, expects a transformation of mundane reality and espouses a gentle pacifistic communitarianism based on apostolic sharing. The hippies share their goods and beg like early Franciscans. On the other hand the bands of hippies are not a disciplined order or sect but a shifting agglomeration of like-minded persons. (Not that the early Franciscans were so very well disciplined!) Their saviour may be Christ but equally might be the legendary King Arthur and Merlin. It seems uncertain whether hope wells up from the sources of goodness deep in the earth, or descends from heaven in traditional manner, perhaps with the help of modern technology in the form of a flying saucer. The pollution from which the pilgrims flee is not merely the moral evil of the City of Destruction and of its concrete jungles, but the scientific pollution of the sacred earth. Indeed the sense of environmental pollution is one of the more lasting residues of the sixties.

This pilgrim devotion to myths intertwined with Christian motifs and partially based on Christian patterns also finds expression in the cult of Tolkien. Tolkien wrote some of his books for children but his adult followers absorb his work as a kind of imaginative shadowing of Christian ideas in which the white power of good confronts the powers of darkness. In Tolkien, therefore, moral categories are restored and the theme of childish innocence is not so much a return to pre-social condition as a re-creation of the New Testament theme of the 'little ones' who enter into the Kingdom of God. It is therefore not far removed from a Christian mysticism which endeavours to see a world conformed to the vision of Isaiah. Nature itself shines as before the Fall and after the Restoration. This condition is not beyond good and evil but envisages the containment of evil. The mythical history envisages the various phases of the battle against darkness and when the light shines it shines on the yeoman virtue of England's green and pleasant land.

Yet it requires only a marginal shift of emphasis for these gentle, idyllic and pastoral themes to be transmuted into darker colours. Not so far from Glastonbury Tor is Silbury Hill, a pre-Christian mound whose origin is unknown, and here the pilgrims seek *power* from the earth as much as they seek goodness. The mystic quest for salvation can switch into the acquisition of magical potencies and once power is invoked the gentle pilgrims can become violent deliverers. Add magic and amoral potency to the Christian myth and there emerges the figure of a Charles Manson: not crucified but crucifying. This figure *inverts* the Christian story: his disciples are his sexual slaves, those who suffer from their activities are victims of the divine. Similar motifs appeared in the notorious child murders known as the 'Moors murders'; they were violent and sadistic, re-enacting a blasphemous model of the crucifixion.

The invocation of the powers of darkness by an inversion of the Christian means of salvation is, of course, an ancient practice. But in its modern forms it has links with magic and Voodoo: the figure of Jimi Hendrix symbolized this link. The invocation of magic and the empathy with African and West Indian cultural forms found its expression in the Afro hairdo. Hair sticking out in all directions signified sexual potency, primitivistic sympathies and alienation from European social control.

Student commitment to irrationality also taps a somewhat different substratum of non-Christian religion: divination and astrology. Since a major motif in student consciousness is immediacy, choice and existential openness, the growing interest in divination is curious. It is even more curious in that one of the most popular forms of divination, the I Ching, belongs to a Chinese civilization where roles were very sharply circumscribed. But, of course, the Taoist undercurrent to Confucian civilization was an anarchistic and quietist nostalgia for the small community, and as such highly congruent with student ideology. So too is the penchant for macrobiotic foods. The really surprising element is the overlap between the culture of the young and educated with the magical aspect of Taoism. However, systems of magic and divination, though not concerned with freedom, do tend to be individualistic. They give a prognosis for personal destiny: they present an impersonal prediction which can be worked to the individual's advantage. Thus we have a paradox: belief in the sacred individual rejects science and its predictions in favour of quasi-science and divination. It also fills in the gap left by the rejection of traditional ways of doing things and by the rejection of moral rules, thus easing what becomes the intolerable burden of existential choice. How much the sections of the youth culture which embrace antinomian anarchy overlap the sections which consult systems of divination is a matter for further study.

The fundamental point underlying all the foregoing analysis has been the tendency to eliminate categories and I will now try to bring together in a highly schematic manner the variety of ways in which categories are undermined. In the first place, the new attitude tries to achieve identity without initially accepting badges of identification whether those of a particular religion or of a country. Then it tries to break down distinctions between fathers and sons: to accept paternalism is as corrupt as identifying with the fatherland. Similarly a religion of the sons rejects heavenly fathers along with earthly fathers: it seeks to be submerged in a totality which engulfs man, nature and God. Man returns to the bosom of nature and sees his unsocialized desires as inherently 'natural'. Nothing is unnatural, except the division of sex and role. Sexual differentiation is seen as imposed by society on an irrelevant biological base: men become feminized and clothing barely distinguishes male from female. Finally, the new female man rejects all categorization of himself in terms of competence and hierarchy: his precious psyche is not to be contaminated by tests or his faculties assessed in a tested hierarchy of qualifications. He is, in fact, a pure person, nothing else but a mortal soul freed from all contingent labels. For him there is neither male nor female, Jew nor Greek, Christian nor pagan, public nor private, sacred nor profane. The only distinction is that between those who have recovered wholeness and personal authenticity and those who have not: the bond and the free. And the old are by definition bond and the young free.

So we may conclude with a double contradiction. Humanistic liberalism has been destroyed in the most paradoxical way by a doctrine of the 'natural' person freely expressing himself in the 'natural' community. The assumption behind this doctrine is a classical liberal notion: the 'invisible hand' harmonizing individual desire and social structures. Religion too has been destroyed in the most paradoxical way: by engulfing the secular in the divine. The former is not possible, the latter not even desirable.[2]

Note

1. Yet, of course, all the 'reforms' desired by radicals required structures of authority and large bureaucracies for their implementation. Since the late sixties there has been a steady increase of bureaucracy in the universities. The student movement as such died, leaving a grey web of rules and examination regulations. It should be emphasized that the current student population (1978) is responsible and tolerant.

2. Most of the above should be read in the past tense.

V

Marxism: Functional Equivalent of Religion?

This particular analysis is centred on one complex issue: the extent to which Marxism can constitute a 'functional equivalent' of religion. In such an analysis we can be aided initially by the advantages and disadvantages which Soviet writers *themselves* impute to Marxism in its struggle with religion. Of course, these writers do not envisage any permanent disadvantages attaching to Marxism, only temporary imperfections in its preaching and application. They note in particular that advantages and disadvantages vary significantly according to the type of religion concerned.

As regards Utopian sectarianism of the kind that organizes itself in self-contained communes Marxism has few disadvantages. This is not necessarily on account of any basic superiority of materialistic over religious forms of communitarian organization since the religious forms were only too successful, but because a utopian community can be eliminated by political decision. The *raison d'être* of religious communitarianism is rooted in discrete communities and these can be regarded as unjustifiable enclaves of autonomous activity in a society which proscribes all such activity. If this activity is also successful it can be eradicated for a second reason: its relative wealth. Thus although Marxist thinking can view religious communitarianism as progressive prior the advent of the revolution, the very consonance between progressive religion and progressive ideology makes the elimination of the former necessary once the revolution is regarded as achieved. The sectarian community has no more chance of survival *as such* than it had in the Middle Ages. It may linger on in Molokan villages or in Doukhobor remnants but the heart of its existence has been plucked out. Not until Marxist society achieves the minimal liberalization such as prevailed in late Tsarist Russia can such communities revive.

As regards the Russian Orthodox Church the balance of appeal and of strength is rather different. The Russian Church is deeply implicated in the most profound currents of Russian thought and in the very existence of the nation. It has by a process of syncretism and assimilation woven its forms into the life of an agrarian society and into many of the rituals of the countryside. Some of these rituals derive from pagan religions long preceding Orthodoxy. Traditional religion is therefore aided by the ancient rhythms of rural life, though disadvantaged by the accretions of superstition. Marxist propaganda can point to the superstitious elements and to primitive semi-magical practices and plausibly suggest that the dogma of Orthodoxy is anti-scientific in its totality.

The Russianness of Orthodoxy is less easily dealt with. The practice of baptism is remarkably widespread, partly because of the emotional depth and aesthetic aura which the Orthodox ritual is able to impart, but also because many Russians still conceive of entry into the Orthodox Church and membership of Russian society as coterminous. Such conceptions are rooted in social forms which conjoin religious and ethnic identity but they have not entirely lost their power for all that. Even if they were to lose their power the connection of Orthodoxy with Russian culture is ineradicable short of a break with the past so drastic as to deprive Russians of access to their own highest achievements: to the act of a Rublev, to Pushkin, Dostoievsky and Tolstoy, to the writings of a Pasternak or Solzhenitsyn. Whereas at lower educational levels Orthodoxy is linked to membership in a culture at higher levels it is linked to full access to that culture.

The present tendency to 'countryside' literature, which includes romanticization of the peasant, is one instance of this. Moreover, when the perfunctory aesthetic expressions of Marxism are lacking in appeal and cosmic grandeur religion is not without resources. The very physical presence of churches, as Solzhenitsyn has noted, is an invitation to alternative modes of awareness currently forbidden. If Orthodoxy sanctifies birth it also imparts meaning even to death. In the long run no political meaning can conceivably be imparted to death apart from laudatory recitals of ideological virtue. Orthodoxy approaches death with a symbolism of light and of Resurrection. Although Marxist apologists accuse the Orthodox faith of pessimism it conceives of a transfiguration of the world and of man which has a profoundly optimistic aspect.

Yet Russia is no longer an agrarian society, even though the agrarian sector remains very large, and in any case the organization of collective farming is done in such a way as to maximize ideological control and the flow of political and atheistic propaganda. More subtle organization of agricultural life can attempt to utilize a folklore separated from its religious associations, such as is embodied in the traditional marriage ceremony which then becomes serviceable as a means to prettify Soviet *rites de passage*. Relatively few marriages are now celebrated in church. Furthermore an organization such as the Orthodox Church requires a visible existence and a priesthood: both of these can be subjected to very severe constrictions. The only limit on the pressure which may be brought to bear is the continued existence of an underground Orthodoxy and the possibility of frustrated Orthodox believers being converted to less visible forms of religion, such as the Baptist faith. An official hierarchy too clearly controlled and too obviously a mere political tool, and an official organization too rapidly run down results in the appearance of clandestine forms much less easy to control and identify. Thus control has to recognize some limits if only to maximize the effects of its own efforts. A pliant official organization is better than a semi-dissident invisible Church.

This dilemma is what Wittvogel called the diminishing marginal returns of bureaucratic centralism. The official Church can use the unofficial Church to help it survive against officialdom.

Perhaps the most viable form of religion in Soviet society is evangelical Protestantism, particularly where it results in a work-ethic highly acceptable to a people deeply concerned with the fulfilment of norms of productivity. The visible organization is minimal and the psychological predisposition not necessarily inimical in any *direct* way to political orthodoxy. It is of course in some degree individualistic, and the elevation of the autonomous person is a cardinal sin by Soviet standards, but this individualism need not and indeed cannot have any overt social expression. Whereas the Orthodox can sometimes be accused of being poor citizens and can even on occasion be labelled drunken citizens, the evangelical Christians and Baptists are good and temperate workers. Nor can the anti-clericalism still extant in Soviet Russia be utilized to blacken their reputation. Only the fact that their co-religionists are to be found in the West and more especially in America, stands to their discredit. And just as it is unwise to make the overt organization of Orthodoxy too clearly a tool of political control so it is even more unwise to do so in the case of the Baptists. Already a sizeable proportion of Baptists adhere to underground forms of their faith and their capacity to fragment into numerous sub-groups meeting only in houses or the forests can easily place them beyond the scope of full political control.

Limited possibilities remain open for sectarians like the Adventists and Jehovah Witnesses or for semi-sectarians of the Pentecostalist variety. Soviet society creates pockets of alienation for which eschatological and millenary faiths have considerable appeal. (Indeed, one must recollect in passing that some of the dissident sections of Orthodoxy have themselves acquired an eschatological tendency.) Sectarians bring up their children in courageous defiance of Soviet socialization, and thereby manage to reproduce age-structures more representative of the age-structure of the population as a whole.

On the other hand their withdrawal from Soviet society, including sometimes the armed forces, is *so* visible that whenever there is persecution they are susceptible to physical elimination. Soviet government does indeed recognize that many sectarians are wells of dissident feeling and the Jehovah's Witnesses in particular are fiercely proscribed. The fate of Pentecostalists is only marginally better. In a society where life is organized so much around norms of political conformity the chances of overt dissidence, even in a religious guise, are not very great.

Such considerations clearly bear on the issue of Marxism as a functional equivalent of religion. But there is another aspect which concerns the degree of morphological similarity between Christianity and Marxism. By the morphology of Marxism I mean its fundamental structure and shape. Religions and ideologies do not normally present a series of discrete responses to given problems item by item but have a clearly defined architecture, however incoherent this may be at grass roots. The capacity of a new structure to replace an old depends in part on the ground plan which the previous structure has laid in the psyche and in the social ideals of a society.

Whether or not a new shape can be imposed on (or derived from) an old one is not simply a matter of similarity. It is more a matter whether or not they can locate a crucial common axis on the basis of which more recalcitrant outliers can be remoulded. For example, Confucianism and Marxism share a common one-dimensionality: they do not conceive either of what is set 'above' society in ultimate judgement nor of a bifurcation in society whereby the spiritual has some region of autonomy. This monistic structure is a crucial axis shared in common and makes the replacement of Confucianism by Chinese Marxism a fairly easy matter. It also allows large incidental sectors of the older system to be incorporated in the new, for example its literary and homiletic style or the sense that China constitutes the whole orbis terrarum. At the same time there is no chance of the older system surviving in its integrity: its crucial organ has been removed and is functioning naturally in another social body. The case of Christianity is quite different: it is very much more close to Marxism in its overall shape than is Confucianism. Indeed, as I shall indicate it shares several axes with Marxism which are of the greatest importance. The utopianism and social idealism of Christianity can even prepare the way for Marxism in a way Confucianism cannot. The revolution of 1905 was led by an Orthodox priest who appealed to the social ideal officially promulgated by Tsarism. When that revolution was met by bullets a process of moral disillusion set in. This moral disillusion is immanent in Christian societies and is part of the process whereby Christianity is its own grave digger.

But Christianity not only initiates its own death but also its resurrection. Because Christianity is dualistic both in terms of the spiritual autonomies it generates and in terms of its ultimate court of appeal it is not coterminous in theory or in historical fact with any social system. It suffers in the breakdown of these systems but their destruction is not necessarily the destruction of Christianity *tout court*. The God of Christianity, even the Almighty Father, is never totally identified with the apex of a social system nor is the truth of Christianity dependent straightforwardly on the moral performances of that system. It is dependent *enough* to suffer severe losses by implication in a system whose moral performance is poor, and, as we have seen, it partly initiates its own suffering by virtue of a contrast always available to those who wish to compare what is actually happening to the ideals Christianity itself espouses. Put in summary form, Christianity is incapable of achieving total, stable dominance, and those very features which are responsible for this are *also* responsible for its capacity to survive the wreck of the social systems in which it is implicated.

The monistic one-dimensionality of the Marxist system can take over a society previously dominated by Christianity, but in spite of the strong structural similarity to Christianity the crucial shared axis is absent. Marxism has no judgement but the judgement of history whereas Christianity repudiates the judgement of history. Marxism has no doctrine of its own failure, either of its failure to conquer the world, or – more important – of its failure when in power to correspond to its own ideals. Its moral psychology posits only a malleability of the human psyche and its attempts to implement that malleability involve totalitarian methods destructive of its own claims to liberate man's potential. Having located all contradictions in structural terms it must contradict itself in trying to eliminate that recalcitrance which is not structural. In any case, its understanding of the complex recalcitrance of structure to the application of its formulae was and is naïve. The very belief that it possessed such formulae in any but the most rudimentary form prevented just that tentative experimentalism and varied creative explorations which would gradually have revealed the specific grain offered by different structures and the ways in which they might be moulded. By claiming prematurely to be science it subverted its claim to be a science at all and ensured its fossilization at a pre-scientific level. So not only did it have no doctrine of 'sin', or a psychology to complement its structural propositions, but that area which it conceived to be its strength, theoretical sophistication and all-embracing scientific truth, was in fact double-edged. It criticized the bifurcations of Christianity: its appeal to ultimate judgements and to spiritual autonomies beyond the provenance of the state, and its susceptibility to religious fissures and sects based on that bifurcation. And it could claim these phenomena merely lay along the lines of geological fault produced by the contradictions of a pre-socialist society. But that bifurcation, that double-nature of Christianity not only lay along those lines of social fault and contradiction but also expressed spiritual autonomies and a need for moral judgement beyond any judgement of history. That judgement was made peculiarly relevant by the totalitarian nature which Marxist society found itself bound to adopt. It may be, of course, that totalitarian society can secure itself against all judgement and all spiritual autonomy by sheer physical repression. What does not die by inanition can be killed. But each attempted murder is also itself the fuel of a further indictment.

The above analysis also indicates the difference between Christianity and Marxism as worked out in relation to oriental despotism. Both doctrines attempted to permeate despotic societies; and the despotism has been more or less continuous apart from minor breaks in the later years of Tsardom. Christianity attempts to work by a feminine and passive mode: altering the content of existing established forms, creating new psychological paradigms, initiating enclaves of limited autonomy in monasteries and sects. This mode has the disadvantage of institutionalizing and harmlessly canalizing alienation, and it legitimates apathy. But it nevertheless sets the self-sanctifying tendencies of established forms against the holiness of God and His saints. If heaven is realized below in the solemn rites of the church, it is only an enclave of the Beatific Vision. Society itself is not conceived as the realization of that vision even where the Byzantine court is itself liturgical in form. But once, as in Marxism, a social movement holds there is no judgement beyond that of history, and once that movement sees itself as that judgement, then the spiritual autonomy of man is organized once-for-all in one mighty masculine thrust to reorganize the whole of existing relations, and it can thereafter brook no autonomous judgement on what it has achieved. Just as an enclave of autonomy, such as monasticism or sectarianism, is limited in social space, so a once-for-all revolution is limited in social time: once achieved it must eliminate all the autonomy which was its own generating force on the ground that it is no longer necessary. Thus while Christianity can be partially assimilated to despotism by canalizing its spiritual energies in ways which partly divert their power into harmless enclaves, Marxism can be totally assimilated to despotism because it is a monistic system, a vast sect whose Beatific Vision is coextensive with its own social boundaries without remainder. Thus the new Marxist Church approximates a universally Established Sect: Third Rome. One more point is relevant at this juncture: Marxism's incapacity to explain its own failures. These failures are often explained in curiously non-structural terms and need to be coped with at grass-roots level by a degree of alcoholic consumption which might lead one to suppose that drink is now the opium of the Soviet people. The failures of Soviet society, politically, agriculturally, industrially, have been explained by a cult-of-personality applied in reverse. The 'great man' theory of history is stood on its head and becomes the 'evil genius' theory of history: Stalin is blamed rather than the theories of Marx and Lenin. The key saints and basic holy scriptures can be left untouched provided the subsidiary saint can be removed from his niche or ejected from his mausoleum. Marx was lucky enough to die before the revolution and Lenin to die shortly after it was achieved. Whereas the great achievements of Soviet society – its basic industrialization and universal education – were in large measure attributed to Stalin – now the failures can also be in large measure attributed to him. And the misery which the system actually brings about at the grass-roots level can be soaked up by alcohol. Soviet apologists, and sociologists of religion, frequently refer to bouts of heavy drinking in which whole communities are from time to time engulfed. Sakharov states that the current consumption is three times as high as in Tsarist Russia. These phenomena persist, they say, when the religious feasts with which they were once associated can barely be remembered. They declare an irreconcilable struggle against such phenomena but, as in the struggle against religion, there are reasons for not fighting the battle *à l'outrance*: not only would victory result in a loss of revenue but a source of convenient oblivion would have been removed. If Marxism is not a full functional equivalent for religion alcohol has to substitute for opium.

Ritual provides a further substitute. When referring to ritual I do not mean the attempts by Soviet authorities to replace Christian feasts and Christian *rites de passage* by Soviet ones. I mean the persistent repetition of the basic formulae of sacred Marxist scriptures in commenting on and explaining the various phenomena of Soviet society. This provides an equivalent of Christian apologetic formulae. One has only to read the production of Marxist scholars concerned with the sociology of religion to note the way in which every other page must be marked by a statement of doctrinal orthodoxy. The 'objective relations' of the new socialist reality must be constantly invoked, the new Soviet man treated like an idol, a god who is a fetish of the imagination, a helpful point of expository reference even though he does not actually exist. The hardest task of exposition arises of course if a new Soviet man actually becomes a prey to religious fantasies without being a survival from the past or a fragment of Kulak psychology, or a loser by the present system or a victim of 'limited social relations'. Like some early Christian apologists Marxist propagandists do not believe that phenomena appropriate to previous periods can leak into their own system or that once properly converted there can be apostasies. The formulae which stand in for explanation are presented, ironically, as the achievements of objective science.

In comparing the shape of Marxism and Christianity we are drawing a kind of literary Venn diagram indicating what is common ground and what is special to each. Of course each of them is rooted in even more basic ground, that of Judaism. By the same token further comparisons are possible between Marxism and Islam. Trevor Ling has made out such a comparison in compelling detail, pointing above all to quasi-military unity of the Muslim brotherhood. But in terms of the themes which have been of particular importance in this discussion one ought particularly to stress the common masculinity of Islam and Marxism. Both have the unity of an army and the military metaphor is never an embarrassment. By contrast to speak of *milites Christi* is to feel a tension. Only in Calvinist Christianity is the tension reduced by an activism and a masculinity which harnesses the power of the almighty Father to accomplish mighty revolutions within the world. In origin the sword of the Christian spirit is placed in contradistinction to the secular arm of principalities and powers. Power is necessary in Christianity but remains morally ambiguous, especially in the area of basic religious symbols. For Marxism there is no ambiguity in power itself and proletarian power acquires unqualified legitimacy. There is no *generalized* peace sentiment in Marxism, only a necessary peace enforced within the area of its dominion, and the use of the word 'peace' as a weapon against those outside its dominion. In passing it may be remarked that neither Marxism nor Christianity in its utopian pacifistic form is equipped to make relevant distinctions between moderate abuse of power and atrocious tyranny.

The profoundly 'feminine' element in the psychological grounding of Christianity leads to a degree of sensuous rapprochement with the world, to some recovery of a harmony between man and nature, and to a margin of passivity in relation to extant structures. This is both political weakness and psychic strength. It enables religion to encompass the area of the personal in a profound manner and gives it a doctrine of suffering. That God became a person in a human family, that the Triune God is a unity of persons, that he cares for every person, defines an area of concern almost absent from Marxism except in the most abstract philosophic terms. It is this element which gives rise to contemporary comment by Marxist spokesmen in the Soviet Union about the depth of experience which can be evoked by Christian *rites de passage* and the incapacity of political ideology and norms of production totally to consume the life of individual persons. This is why young revolutionaries in the West are forced back upon the humanism of the early Marx. The Christian and in particular the Protestant emphasis on individuality here finds an area where political ideology has little relevance.

Along with this margin of passivity, femininity, peaceability, acceptance, goes a doctrine of suffering. The acceptance of suffering may become apathy and rejection of the means which are available to reduce it; and the notion of the wages of sin may be used to justify such apathy. But suffering demands an interpretation and the religion of a suffering God, while it cannot explain suffering, can set it within a cosmic context. The suffering of man and the crucifixion of human idealism are fused in the single paradigm of the wounded God. The figure of the crucified, suffering God enters relatively late into the iconography of European art. It is not as easily assimilated as icons of God's power. Even the most Promethean achievements and aspirations in medicine and social engineering are unlikely to reduce the relevance of such a fusion. The abstract paradigmatic figures associated with Soviet (and scientistic) Prometheanism are very different from a concentrated, personal paradigm of human loss and suffering: a hero of the revolution is sharply contrasted with a martyr for the faith. This does not mean of course that heroism in the revolutionary cause does not draw upon the psychic well that has been sunk in Christian cultures round about the concept of martyrdom. The availability of the concept of martyrdom is just another of these areas where Christianity can prepare the way for paradigms which are very opposed to its own. The Christian halo set around martyrdom has again and again allowed an aura to be set about political and social dissent.

Another area is the common emphasis on the charismatic status of the poor although in Christianity the emphasis is on *voluntary* poverty as well as on the simple ineluctable condition of poverty. In other words the moral value of renunciation can be contrasted with the Marxist exhortation to expropriate the expropriators. Yet the Christian doctrine of poverty and equality and its condemnation of riches is one of the psychological slipways along which the revolution may be launched. As George Steiner has argued, a civilization soaked in the ritual repetition of the gospels has been prepared for revolution however much renunciation has deflected action and however often divine legitimation has been invoked to consecrate social structures directly contrary to it. Longfellow's poem about King Robert of Sicily was right to comment on the paradox of an established liturgy celebrating a God who 'hath thrown down the mighty from their seat and exalted them of low degree'. 'Robert of Sicily, brother of Pope Urbane', was right to find the Magnificat objectionable.

In comparing the shape of Marxism and Christianity I have so far concentrated on differences which may allow Christianity continued relevance in Marxist societies and on the structural and psychological slipways of revolution which Christianity has gradually built at the base of European culture. Beyond that, however, one must note the sheer familiarity of the new shape in terms of the old with respect to other areas where the *content* of that shape may be very different. I mean the concept of stages in world history, the emphasis on the word, the notion of a faithful who accept and outsiders who reject, the offer of an either/or for decision one way or the other.

In this whole discussion I have laid particular weight on the sphere of the personal as exposed to Christianity in Marxist society. The very urge to total politicization *could* make a stress on individuality doubly important. Marxism defines those outside its fold as non-persons, rooted in unreality. Their attempts to retain an area of ontological validity in the private sphere are exposed to philosophical denigration and to organized social processes and pressures which define them as enemies of society to be rehabilitated. This is one of the roles of Soviet psychiatry in which the rights of Protestant conscience or the liberal distinction of public and private are labelled pathology. Individuality is not defended solely by religion, but since liberalism is even more condemned in Soviet society religion may provide a viable enclave in which it finds refuge. In any case the liberal bifurcation of public and private is in part a translation of the Christian bifurcation of sacred and secular, and the two concepts which have in the past warred against each other may in a Marxist context find mutual reinforcement, plus whatever elements of Marxist humanism filter through the interstices of official ideology. It is here that the intellectual protest within the Soviet Union finds some margins of overlap with the religious protest.

The main weapon against the individual is comprehensive

mystification and indeed the whole Soviet Union is organized for the mystification, in a Marxist sense, of its own population. Mystification is necessary to defend the privileges of those who control and exercise patronage and to defend all the incursions on personal liberty (like freedom of movement internally and externally) and on the dissemination of information. On the latter point even natural disasters are played down or just not mentioned as a kind of ritual *lèse-majesté* against the might of Soviet Man. Marxist societies are organized like vast sects and are an instance of 'limited social relations' on an enormous scale, preventing information leakages and defections from and to sister Marxist sects, let alone to the western world.

It is a paradox that a system which claimed that the beginning of all criticism was the criticism of religion should have ended up with a form of religion which was the end of all criticism. This situation is in part due to the fact that, contrary to the main thrust of its own self-understanding and predictions, Marxism has been the agent of the industrial revolution rather than the midwife of its advanced potentialities. It would be possible, as I have suggested, to stand the Communist Manifesto on its head and apply its moral critique to the Soviet Union. The power nexus dominates relations between man and man. The status of a human being is that of a mere tool in the creation of basic industries and prestige products and in the fulfilment of production norms for the advantage of future generations and for the greater glory of the state. Man is separated from his product: the personal relation to the soil is depersonalized though an impersonal collectivism dominated by distant bureaucratic heads. The will of people passes through so many centralized mediations that its expression appears to them in a completely alienated form; that alienation is mystified by the claim that it is the will of the people, even when vast masses of actual persons are its abject subjects. The alienation of the product of the intellectual is even more marked: he is organized against himself, his own product is the means of his self-alienation. All criticism is defined as anti-Soviet activity, an offence against the embodiment of proletarian revolution. By virtue of restoring the 'sacred canopy' of an ideological monopoly, such a system becomes a potent vehicle of alienation through the institution of total socialization. Similarly the separation of men from their product, whether it is the product of hand or brain, is a further vehicle of alienation. The manipulators of this system are intellectuals who have transformed themselves into priests. They represent the most deadly of all unions, which is the union of knowledge and power and virtue. In principle such a union seems very desirable but in practice it is uniquely repressive. It was the ancient virtue of Christianity to emphasize the ambiguity of power and the corruption attendant on knowledge. Both the ambiguity and the corruption are well illustrated in the Soviet Union. Explicit ideologies of alienation are uniquely efficient agents of repression.

VI

Religion and the Second Millennium

I have been asked to look forward twenty-five years to the end of the second millennium. A quarter of a century is only a short period in the usual scale of human history and there was a time when prediction might not have been too hazardous. But now the whole face of the world changes within a generation and the prophet is reduced either to mere extrapolation or to imaginative guesses based on alternative scenarios that might reverse or mutate the apparent trends of the moment. I shall concentrate on these apparent trends.

I propose to concern myself with the fate of religion, with the likely prospects for political dogma, and with the possibility of an indifference which is both political and religious. I begin with religion and so doing make only one passing remark. Christianity in 1975 is very differently placed from what it was in 975. In that year it held a tiny segment of the globe and had made only the most limited impact on the pagan and magical substratum of belief which underlay the official clothing of Christian ideology. Now Christianity is in a period of partial recession after the most massive expansions in its whole history. It is decreasingly used to provide the official ideological clothing of the state. The pagan or magical substratum is resurgent and is reinforced by heavy importations from religions across the old boundaries of Christendom. Christianity no longer has a closed frontier with the outside world. In both periods it has just about held the West against the massive depredations of a military and militant opponent: Islam in the past, Marxism in the present.

Christianity faces indifference, magic, nationalism, liberalism, scientism and Marxism. Each is immensely powerful and each enters into alliances with Christianity, sometimes at the level of substance, sometimes at the level of tactical advantage. Each of the major 'isms' colludes with each of the others, or at least represents itself as the fulfilment of the promise found in the others. Marxism and nationalism are in a period of rampant confidence; liberalism and Christianity and scientism in a mood of chastened uncertainty. Christianity colludes with nationalism against Marxism and in a minor way also against liberalism; Christianity suspends its war with liberalism so that both may fight Marxism; Marxism fights scientism on the ground that it alone is the true science and proceeds to reduce Christianity to magic and liberalism to ideology on the same basis. Marxism colludes with nationalism in both East and West. In the West it may collude with any nationalism, even one already colluding with Christianity, if by so doing it can disrupt the West internally. In the East it only colludes with that hegemonic nationalism which assists its dominance and denies all nationalisms which fragment that dominance, especially if they also collude with Christianity. Tactics vary of course according to the varied opposing strengths. Czech and Lithuanian nationalism are not tolerated; Polish nationalism has to be.

In a way it is possible to argue that the modern period shows, and will show, that only two sociological prophets have been seriously validated by the condition of the modern world: Durkheim and Weber. The seeming success of Marxism as an ideology has been the partial eclipse of Marx, just as the success of Christianity as an ideology led to the partial eclipse of Christ. Durkheim laid his finger on one enormously powerful factor: the identity of a people expressed in its language and its myth, whether that myth be one of messianic triumph or messianic suffering. The strength of Marxism is partly rooted in the power of messianic nationalism; Christianity, too, is strong in so far as it is linked to the national myth. By the same token the weakness of Christianity arises as it faces a world dominated by the Weberian scenario of technical and bureaucratic rationality. It is that same bureaucratic and technical rationality which subverts the core of Marxism even as the Marxist élites are forced to use it to extend and consolidate their power. A weaker if purer Christianity emerges, but in so far as it is weaker it necessarily gives way to indifference. A stronger and more corrupt Marxism emerges, but in so far as it is more corrupt it creates either indifference or a purely passive acceptance. So Christianity either colludes with nationalism, assimilates liberalism or retreats before technical, bureaucratic rationality. And Marxism colludes with certain nationalisms, rejects liberalism and is subverted by technical bureaucratic rationality. The giant strength lies with technical, manipulative reason (of which magic is the parody) and with the power of collective identity: nationalism. Such is the present scenario.

Now I want to look a little closer at the precise concatenation of these collusive rivals within the West and the East. By dividing my analysis into two sections I implicitly deny what I may seem to have already affirmed, which is the unity of East and West under the joint hegemony of technical rationality and nationality. It makes an enormous difference whether or not power is focused and centralized and unambiguously legitimated in the style of Marxist states or partially focused and ambiguously legitimated according to the present Western style. Monopoly and oligopoly share certain common elements in that they are neither of them systems of pure ideological pluralism and evenly dispersed power. But one makes an approach to dispersion and pluralism which the other does not, and this is the strength and the weakness both of Western oligopoly and Eastern monopoly. It will give rise to a fundamental question: can Western liberalism fight its own internal logic of increasing pluralism in order not to weaken itself *vis-à-vis* the militant monopoly power of Marxism and yet retain the kind of strength which derives from the fact that it has at least been partially true to its own promise? Of course, the position of Christianity over and against this single question will be that of an awkward intruder and powerless referee in a major fight. In so far as pluralism succeeds, religion becomes one option among many; in so far as monopoly succeeds it is altogether excluded from the monopoly.

The present condition of the West, ideologically and religiously, is curious. There is a movement towards homogeneity which is countered by a movement to diversity. The two movements are not, of course, merely contradictory but symbiotic. The metropolitan centres expand and push against the peripheries, which absorb, or contract or resist. The confrontation of centre with periphery could be described as a tension between the universalistic cosmopolitan criteria of liberalism, for which no ascriptive criterion is relevant, and the particularistic criteria of nationalism, centred in ethnicity and language. There is, of course, a definitional and historical awkwardness about such a formulation since liberalism has included tendencies to virulent nationalism. Nevertheless, there is a significant cosmopolitanism, ensconced in the great metropolitan centres, which corrodes the sense of locality and local loyalty, undermines dialect speech and minority languages and espouses a functional morality hostile to irrational taboo and suprarational sanctity. This mentality is mobile, shifting, hedonistic, technicist, more capable of activating rights than inculcating duties. It has no sense of personal guilt and yet possesses an enlarged excoriating sense of collective sin. Thus individual wrong-doers are not responsible in a moral sense, but collective wrong-doers – structures and cultures – *are* responsible. The responsibility is both moral and causal. Given the rise of this particular form of guilt, sanctions against rebels decline and guilt unnerves the confidence of the élite, especially in the professional and academic sector. The overall consequence is an odd alternation between hedonistic fare provided for the majority (bread and circuses) and a self-conscious collective moral masochism practised by the minority. The system runs into serious trouble once either the bread and circuses are in short supply or its moral performance fails to satisfy the masochistic criteria of part of the élite. In short, the cosmopolitan system propagated from the centre, with no other focus of meaning than the abstract concept of citizenship and of citizen rights, and with no other basis of legitimacy than performance, is unstable. It is both unstable and it expands and therefore it extends the sector of instability. Its symbols are dirtied by poor moral performance *relative to expectation*, its myths downgraded by criticism, its sacred places emptied of the numinous, its rhetoric deprived of resonance.

These tendencies can be overstated, because underneath moves the undertow of ancient pieties and respects: to churches, sacred persons, holy nations and cenotaphs, ceremonials and historical myths. Nevertheless the acid is evident and powerful, and acts to corrode the basis of liberalism's own existence and power. The cosmopolitan liberal ethos has a great power for self-destruction, because the hole in the heart and head allows back all kinds of irrational nostrums which re-occupy parts of the metropolis, and because the ancient pieties which have been threatened stir uneasily and powerfully along the cultural and geographical margins. The metropolis is besieged by cults taking over the ideological space evacuated by Christianity, and the cultural margins become infected by virulent local nationalisms in partial collusion with Christianity and/or whatever political dogma is opposed to the political coloration of the centre. The Basque example is the most obvious; Croatia provides an Eastern instance.

Now I will take each of the elements just mentioned and deal with them in turn, noting the distribution of the varied kinds of collusion referred to earlier. What then is the symbiosis of forces in the contemporary West? Here are some representative combinations:

Christianity plus nationalism plus deviant political dogma
Christianity plus nationalism minus deviant political dogma
Nationalism plus political dogma minus Christianity

Christianity plus liberalism minus nationalism
Liberalism plus nationalism minus Christianity

I could amplify the list to include such elements as magic and superstition or the penchant for experiential and mystical cults, but the sets of combinations would become uselessly complicated, as well as invalidated by the existence of overlapping definitions. All that is needed is a specification of certain crucial combinations: one dominant on the periphery, another at the centre.

I begin at the periphery where the sense of sub-cultural identity stirs uneasily at the threat posed by the tentacles of the liberal cosmopolitan centre. The periphery fears the instability induced by the messages from the centre, though for the centre this fear and this 'reaction' is just another indication of instability. The periphery may be primarily religious or primarily linguistic and ethnic, or it may include some combination of these. To the extent that each is present then there is mutual reinforcement. Ethnicity, language, religion each exist in a symbiotic unity which, if reinforced by deviant politics, is made even more resistant to outside pressure. Thus in the Basque country each element shores up every other in spite of this, an apparent contradiction between the deviant political dogma and the deviant religious intensity of the area. The tendency noted elsewhere for religion to become separated off from ethnicity or linguistic community becomes checked in these situations of cultural defence. The Basque country exemplifies a maximal combination which is assisted by such factors as geographical peculiarity, and the genuine possibility of economic and political autonomy. A minimal combination is found in parts of Sweden where the *only* element in cultural defence is religious, or in those parts of provincial England where a sense of alienation from the moral and religious indifferentism of the metropolis gives power to movements like the Festival of Light. An intermediate combination is found in the Bergen hinterland where deviant religion, a dialect variant and ancient economic and cultural distinctiveness each assist the other. Other examples abound: Catalonia, Galicia, Brittany, the Alto Adige, North Jutland, Scotland, Ireland and Wales, Northern Holland, the Jura and Flanders.

The underlying point is simple. As we approach the second millennium the national pieties of the centre have lost colour and blood, and have stimulated the national and religious identities of the periphery. The partial separation of religion and national identity at the centre is checked at the periphery partly *because* the separation *is* so characteristic of the centre. So secularity and universality are countered by particularity and by the religious. No doubt, as time goes on, the different areas of sub-cultural assertiveness will either spiral towards autonomy where the maximal combinations exist, or spiral towards a weakness expressed only in symbolic shreds and tatters.

But more remains to be said about the centre because even there magic, mysticism, the functionality of the Protestant Ethic, civic piety and the union of nation and religion, retain some power, even in certain instances reviving power. Let us first take national and civic piety, then magic and mysticism, and finally the Protestant Ethic, that is, work and duty.

Magic and mysticism re-occupy some parts of the centre. They represent respectively a manipulative attitude to the universe parodying science, and an expressivist preference, whereby religious experience is deprived of dogmatic reference and of institutional location. The return of magic is less a return than a revival. Magic was partly assimilated and partly attacked by Christianity, but never eliminated. Nowadays it breaks free of its collusion with Christianity and asserts itself in partial opposition to religion. Astrology and even witchcraft represent unverified and unconventional varieties of science and scientific prediction, and so long as science is inadequate so long pseudo-science provides the cognitive system of the gaps. The mechanistic model provided by science may even incline some to believe that manipulation by a quasi-science based on the deterministic mechanistic premise is probably superior to prayer.

Meanwhile, the other function of prayer, meditation and communion, is partly taken over by mysticism. The object of prayer, in the form of a personal God, is transmuted into the eternal ground of Being. Just as science has a shortfall so the experiential possibilities of modern society are constricting and liable to breed a desire for ecstasy. The desire to leap over the restrictions of normality often combines with the need to conquer anonymity. This combination brings about the potent union of mysticism and the nostalgia for community. Bureaucratic anonymity breeds parodies of itself in astrology, and creates powerful opponents in the joint forces of mysticism and community.

Meanwhile the more conventional Christian prayer persists, largely in petitionary form, and a Christian version of mystical community appears in the form of charismatic and Pentecostal movements. The ancient pieties of private prayer, limited moral reciprocity, civic and national duty remain, even though attenuated. But they are split between a *very private* religion at the level of the individual, based on duty and a vague concept of the origin and source of all things, and a civic cult centring around the symbols of local pride and national identity. Those symbols may be the British monarchy or the French notion of the nation as metaphysical mistress of all Frenchmen. Whatever their particular form, such symbols represent universal reservoirs of power by no means easily used up. They are usually supported by myths relating to democracy, liberty and fraternity et cetera, which are either played down because their realization is recognized as incomplete or else taken so literally as to breed rebellion against their lack of concrete embodiment. Even so, all these myths and symbols retain considerable influence, and there seems no reason why they should not continue to do so. Indeed, if the current denigration of myth and symbol continues it should activate a counter-attack since the centre of modern society *cannot* subsist on mere technical rationality.

A reaction in favour of overreaching myth and symbol may be complemented by a partial return of the 'Protestant Ethic'. A society where duty has been dissolved in personal advantage and where efficiency has been converted to the vagaries of personal feeling is on the road to ruin. Those who repudiate efficiency and work are themselves on the road to downward social mobility, thereby allowing those who still respect work and efficiency to take their places. Moreover, in all the vast technical sub-structure of modern society an addiction to pure personal vagary cannot be tolerated. Reliability and time-keeping and the work ethic are all essential to the social fabric, including the very existence of those who reject the work ethic. So we may argue, as Peter Berger has done, that there are limits to both magic and personal vagary because the dictates of technical rationality can only allow such to flourish in the private sphere.

Having thus characterized the symbioses, continuities and mutations found in the contemporary West a different concatenation of the basic alternatives and tendencies may be observed in the East. I shall begin by repeating the analysis of periphery and centre, but this time not from the perspective of a corrosive and expanding pluralism but of a corrosive and expanding monopoly.

Many sociologists and many liberals, not to mention many liberal sociologists, believe that privatization, individualism and pluralism are the inherent tendencies of the modern world. For them the monopoly observed in the East is either illusory or temporary. In fact, in so far as methods of control become less physical, direct, and brutal, that may merely reflect the ability of the system to produce conformity by internal assent as well as by external compliance.

There is no reason why an ideological monopoly which controls the state apparatus and the socialization process should give up its power, particularly as such power only contradicts the content of the ideology at a sophisticated rather than a superficial level. A liberal monopoly of power is plainly inconsistent, even maybe the very idea of socialization into the norms of tolerance, but a Marxist monopoly of power can represent itself plausibly as the vehicle of proletarian will.

Indeed, to the extent that it has power it can make that plausibility stick. It may even be that the élite believes its own myth, by contrast to many élite members in the West who only believe in the *ideal* promulgated by their myth.

But temporarily, of course, the Marxist myth (which illustrates both a myth of power and the power of myth) will descend to tactical variations in policy according to circumstance. The fundamental tactical requirement is to follow whatever is necessary to service the alliance between those who maintain the apparatus and certain élite sectors of the working class in the key heavy industries. Nothing else is necessary once this tactical requirement is satisfied. The 'intelligentsia' and key sector workers together benefit differentially from the system and their leaders distribute the basic currency of power and patronage in return for compliance.

The one tactical mistake which must not be made, and which will not be made, is any important concession to ideological rivalry, private opinion and decentralization. Decentralization concedes footholds to deviant nationalisms; ideological pluralism allows religion and criticism on religious premises; and private opinion dissolves and nibbles at the dogmas which shore up monopoly power. In not making such a mistake communist élites are assisted by the universal tendency of modern society towards centring power in the state and in well organized collectives and pressure groups. Since in the West the pressure groups partially neutralize each other, some scope and influence remains for private opinion, but in the East all the pressure groups are compounded into one, leaving the single citizen facing the unified state, the single union, the homogeneous 'conscience collective'.

Religion is, of course, legally privatized and organizationally cut down to the minimum. Nationalism similarly is not tolerated *per se*, but used selectively as the vehicle of hegemony. And yet there are significant variations, which have sufficient structural root to last at least up to the second millennium. Thus, in Poland, the millenary union of Christianity and nationhood is so powerful that the communist rulers are both pragmatic enough and patriotic enough to tolerate it, even though they take such measures as push religion in the *direction* of a private association. Similarly in Romania the Latin and special nature of the nation has been historically carried by the Church, and to destroy those roots prematurely would destroy the nation. Being at the frontier with the Russian imperium Romania and Poland have a strong motive to defend their particularity even at the expense of accepting a role for religion. The Durkheimian urge to identity shows its power yet again. At the other end of the spectrum the powerful union of nationality and of Roman Catholic religion in Lithuania will be broken up because it offends the hegemony of Russian nationalism. The Croatian urge to religious and national integrity will be curbed (and decentralization halted) because it threatens the wider national unity and sentiment. In Albania religion will be crushed because it is even more fissiparous than in Yugoslavia and can be plausibly associated with foreign influence and culture.

It is in Albania, if anywhere, that the first truly atheist state will emerge. The function of religious myth will have been transferred to a virulent nationalistic Marxism for which all ideological variation or private faith is tantamount to treason. Here, of course, we note a paradox and a qualification. The paradox is that the unifying umbrella of religion, the sacred canopy of Berger's analysis, is here restored under the aegis of a self-defined scientific and secular ideology. The single ideological universe and the Inquisition come back in secular disguise. Their association with Christianity was purely contingent, whereas their association with the secular ideology of Marxism is logical. The *myth* of science, socially embodied, leads to its own closure and the wheel comes full circle. Indeed this can even happen in the West in that the paradigms and powers of science are accepted *de fide* by large groups of the population, but this mild degree of closure never goes any further than the labelling of those with the old-time faith as deviant and peculiar. Perhaps it is worth remarking at this point that both in East and West the demarcation of the deviant in terms of labels derived from science, especially psychiatry, is a growing tendency. Scientific truth, like religious faith, once socially embodied, inevitably enters into the processes of social control. But in the West this is patchy and indirect, in the East direct and almost universal. All the phenomena supposedly peculiar to religion: citation of sacred texts, labelling of deviants, nihilation of cognitive minorities, and processes of orthodoxy, schism and heresy, make their bow once more in the garb of secular ideology. Hence religion will not only be pushed into the private sphere but to the extent that it emerges will demand that the humane possibilities suppressed within the Marxist orthodoxy will be realized, just as secular criticism once demanded that Christianity deliver those goods which it hid beneath the robes of priestcraft. The signs of this critical role are already evident both in West and East. In the one it will flourish, thereby both weakening and strengthening the West, in the other it will be suppressed, especially if it makes any common cause either with liberals or the Marxist left. Christianity will in any case be pushed to the margins: the lower and peripheral sectors of society, to the countryside, to the women and the less educated, and to the frustrated national groupings. It will survive most easily either amongst 'the dregs' as defined by socialist society or as a 'Protestant Ethic' of the moderately educated like the Baptists. After all work and discipline are useful to industrial society.

The monopolistic system is itself, of course, a form of verbal magic, which is powerful because believed. But when people observe the discrepancy between ideal and performance they either turn again to religion, which recognizes just that discrepancy, or they sink into cynicism. Those sectors dominated by bureaucratic rationality supplement such cynicism with a technicism, an ideological indifference, and a hedonistic, instrumental attitude not unlike that in the metropolitan West. To that extent there is and will be a convergence. The consequences of a hedonistic attitude are already easily observed in the Soviet Union, and a country like Czechoslovakia serves to exemplify the dull apathy of existential and national defeat. Marxism is conspicuous in its failure to fill the needs of the private and personal dimension and either religion or hedonism flow back to fill the vacuum left by an ideology which is both too public and too Puritan.

The year 2000 will either exemplify all these tendencies or it will not. Forgive me, but I know no more than I know, and prediction can only peter out in tautology. I can predict here and predict there, and I hope such predictions are clear enough from the remarks and generalization above. I only make one secure prediction which is premised at least on the survival of sectarian religion, both in East and West. As the year 2000 approaches men will go up into the mountains to await the ending of the ages, when the Lord returns either in clouds of glory or, as befits a technical age, in a cosmic vehicle. And if those sectarian enthusiasts are lucky they will be disappointed, but given the buildup of social forces and technical capacities, however these warm up and cool off politically from time to time, they could turn out to be right. After all, the development of secular powers has brought both utopia and doom closer to sober reality than ever before.

Perhaps some final remarks are worthwhile about the survival or revival of Christianity. Throughout this essay I have discussed Christianity in alliance with something else, liberalism or nationalism or conservatism, and, I might have said, socialism. Gradually, however, Christianity has shifted out of its ancient alliances with other forces: the alliance with conservatism and statism has clearly broken up; the collusion with liberalism is under strain, and the expanding *entente cordiale* with socialism is marred by the inheritance of anti-clericalism and the crucial issue of education. Where Christianity has taken a liberal aspect it has faced those corrosions of liberalism which undermine its own profoundest insights, limit its realism, and make it more tentative than proclamatory, more a cultural gloss than a prophetic judgement. This is how Christianity has succumbed to a religiously toned form of the *bien pensant* style. So both conservative politics and liberal culture have been partially separated off from Christianity, and socialism in its turn has explicitly confined religion to the sphere of the private.

In that private sphere it does of course meet the profound existential tensions of existence with a mythology of celebration, consolation and judgement, and a symbolic transmutation of the axes of human life: the redemptive birth, the holy community, the heavenly city, tragic death, the promise of new life. The vulnerable child and the dying man are paradigms of human predicament and divine possibility which have in the past suffered necessary translation into the vocabulary of hierarchy, false promise, delusion and passivity: in short, alienation. It may be that as the contradictions of liberalism and socialism reveal themselves as inherent and as Christianity can be seen distinct from either, that a celebration of a community yet to be fully realized, a recognition of a tragedy written in the nature of life, and of a hope not exhausted by the necessary imperfection of social arrangements, will seem once again relevant. Religion has to find a way of detaching itself from liberalism without contributing to the defeat of freedom and tolerance, and of distinguishing itself from socialism without being thrown directly into the arms of socialism's enemies or denigrating the impulse to the equalization of human opportunities. What can be said is that in different ways and different contexts the year 2000 is bound to see a failure to hold such difficult tensions and yet enough success to take Christianity alive into the rest of the century.